AF252056

THE OTHER GUY

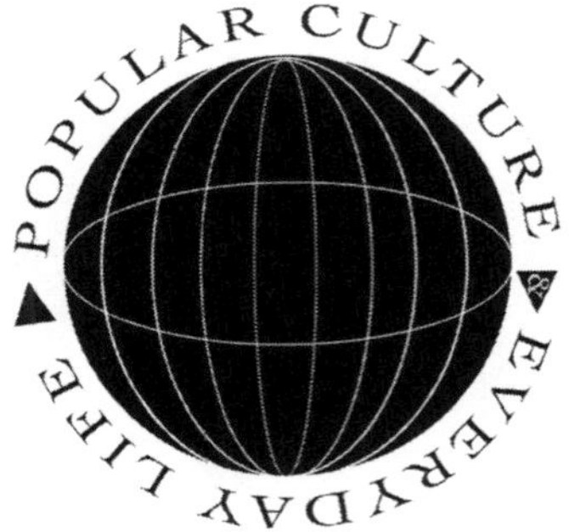

Toby Miller
General Editor

Vol. 26

The Popular Culture and Everyday Life series
is part of the Peter Lang Media and Communication list.
Every volume is peer reviewed and meets
the highest quality standards for content and production.

PETER LANG
New York • Bern • Frankfurt • Berlin
Brussels • Vienna • Oxford • Warsaw

Derek A. Burrill

THE OTHER GUY

MEDIA MASCULINITY WITHIN THE MARGINS

PETER LANG
New York • Bern • Frankfurt • Berlin
Brussels • Vienna • Oxford • Warsaw

Library of Congress Cataloging-in-Publication Data

Burrill, Derek A.
The other guy: media masculinity within the margins / Derek A. Burrill.
pages cm. — (Popular culture and everyday life; Vol. 26)
Includes bibliographical references and index.
1. Masculinity in mass media. I. Title.
P96.M385B87   791.43'653—dc23   2014024783
ISBN 978-1-4331-2246-0 (hardcover)
ISBN 978-1-4331-2245-3 (paperback)
ISBN 978-1-4539-1428-1 (e-book)
ISSN 1529-2428

Bibliographic information published by **Die Deutsche Nationalbibliothek**.
Die Deutsche Nationalbibliothek lists this publication in the "Deutsche
Nationalbibliografie"; detailed bibliographic data are available
on the Internet at http://dnb.d-nb.de/.

Cover image: still from *Admission* (2013), directed by Paul Weitz, showing Paul Rudd.
© Focus Features; used courtesy of Photofest.

The paper in this book meets the guidelines for permanence and durability
of the Committee on Production Guidelines for Book Longevity
of the Council of Library Resources.

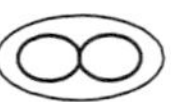

© 2014 Peter Lang Publishing, Inc., New York
29 Broadway, 18th floor, New York, NY 10006
www.peterlang.com

All rights reserved.
Reprint or reproduction, even partially, in all forms such as microfilm,
xerography, microfiche, microcard, and offset strictly prohibited.

Printed in the United States of America

For Bekah

CONTENTS

ACKNOWLEDGMENTS

I want to thank the team at Peter Lang for their valuable feedback and guidance, particularly Mary Savigar, who has been a manager, hand-holder and friend, and Sophie Appel, who generously put up with my eccentricities and anxieties. Additionally, I would like to thank Toby Miller for his guidance and editorial expertise—I will continue to aspire to your level of work and commitment to social justice and academic distinction. Finally, I would like to thank the countless people that talked with me about their experiences with gender and sexuality, particularly the men who are striving to be more thoughtful, kind and progressive.

INTRODUCTION

No, not that guy. The *other* guy

The male subject's aspirations to mastery and sufficiency are undermined from many directions—by the Law of Language, which founds subjectivity on a void; by the castration crisis; by sexual, economic, and racial oppression; and by the traumatically unassimilable nature of certain historical events.[1]

—Kaja Silverman, *Male Subjectivity at the Margins*

In a 2013 article published in *The Onion*, a long-standing satirical newspaper akin to the reportage on *The Daily Show with Jon Stewart*, the headline read: "Area Man Unsure if He's Male-Bonding or Being Bullied." The article continues:

Perplexed local man Russell Chambliss has no idea if the coworkers seated with him at Malone's Irish Tavern are attempting to forge a male bond with him or cruelly harassing him, the 26-year-old shipping clerk told reporters Wednesday evening. "When Bill called me 'limp dick' and punched my shoulder, I wasn't sure if he was insulting me or just being friendly, but everyone else was smiling and laughing so I smiled back," said Chambliss, adding that he has also been called "fucker" several times, which feels like bullying even though the whole group seems to be referring to one another as "fucker."[2]

If you haven't met one yet, Russell Chambliss is a useful representation of the central masculine figuration in this book, the *other guy*, a dude stuck in the in-between, distinctly unable to be 'one of the guys,' consistently befuddled by the constant push-pull of the homosocial and the homophobic.

In an equally humorous and telling manner, halfway into the 2013 Emmy Awards, Hollywood actor and comedian Will Ferrell appeared onstage, presumably to serve as an award presenter. Shuffling distractedly toward the microphone, his three real-world children (all boys) in tow, Ferrell looked embarrassed, particularly to be wearing shorts, a t-shirt and sandals. Thoroughly frazzled as he lined his kids up beside him, he launched into his cue-card lines with all the zeal of an exhausted parent, hitting all the characterizations of the overwhelmed and perplexed dad with subtle detachment. Before he could finish his lines, he was interrupted by his boys whispering to him, answering them with, "No, you cannot play *Angry Birds* right now. Just share the tablet. Take turns. 30 second turns." Ferrell then explained to the audience why he was looking so out-of-sorts, "There was a cancelation, so they called me literally 45 minutes ago. Um…and, I couldn't find child-care. We had a soccer game. There was a neighbor's birthday party, a nut allergy… I didn't have time to do my hair. It doesn't matter. It's great to be here." He then looked at his kids confusedly, asking "Why are you laughing?" It was a funny moment, touching and a bit sad, but certainly familiar. Will Ferrell, despite his hulking, comedic physique, is often cast in the other guy role, from the much-too-late coming-of-age comedy *Step Brothers* (2008) to the crime comedy, *The Other Guys* (2010). His generally clueless and casually congenial film characters have clearly proven endearing enough that he has worked it into his real-life shtick. Ferrell, as the other guy who shows up to the Emmy Awards in his Saturday morning clothes, also illustrates the intermediated nature of other guyness; he's as much a product of his social scene as he is the silver screen.

While portraying men as clueless in the media is certainly a familiar tactic, these two instances, both fictive in a sense, are rather pregnant portrayals of the new masculine cluelessness. These guys are just trying to figure out the world around them, seemingly flummoxed and confounded, but basically *nice*. However, the other guy is also a performance, and a reactive one at that—these fellas are tactical about their masculinity, constantly strategizing ways to circumvent, obfuscate and deny traditionally masculine behavior and mores, playing the victim here, the drop-out there, yet always begrudgingly acknowledging their own alterity in relation to the alpha male and the tough guy, as well as to women in general (though certainly less often).

The other guy is, at its most basic, a masculine figuration, an idea of masculinity that is historically and culturally situated, reflecting prevailing attitudes about men and men's bodies. Yet, the other guy is also a real man in the real world that is attempting to navigate the shifting narratives of men and women, men and other men and men as representation, chiefly in various forms of the media. The other guy, most often white and middle class, is not the alpha male, not the one who wins first. He is instead more akin to the beta male (and sometimes the omega male), the 'nice guy,' the friend of other, more authoritative men, guys who are not threatened by him and seek him out for advice and solace. He is a friend to women, but not the romantic lead in the traditional sense—if he 'gets the girl' (or, sometimes, the boy), he does so by careful, sincere labor, not through competition. So, in this sense, the other guy is a legacy of the men featured in films from the Golden Age of Hollywood, but not from the Greatest Generation (whose silent stoicism runs counter to the more garrulous, congenial sensibilities of the other guy). James Stewart is perhaps one of the original other guys, with his patient and pater-familial ways, gently cajoling his leading ladies into romantic love and slapping his friends on the back in good-hearted camaraderie. The other guy need not be straight, although the bulk of the media representations that feature him show him to be straight. He's not lascivious, but he can be romantic. He's okay with sex, but he's not sexual. In many ways, the other guy is the straight male version of compromise in the face of great changes—from the rising status of women in culture, to the conscientious acknowledgment of their complicity in the objectification and degradation of these women, from the new, middle-class, economic hardships, to the dizzying array of product choices aimed at the male consumer. In this sense, the other guy as figuration is a form of gender and sexual reparation, so that his masculinity is, at its core, deeply regretful and melancholic, cognizant of male privilege, but often unable or unwilling to rectify the situation. The other guy is apologetic, but how deep does this apologetics go? Or is the other guy another male performance, a strategy employed to get what he wants?

Men's bodies are also significant to this equation, particularly since the other guy's body is second-rate at best, particularly in comparison to the chiseled chest of the primetime hunk. While not obese, the other guy isn't quite a fit body either—the casual approach to body sculpting is the other guy's most understated weapon (for these men still do fight, but through videogames and reality-TV shows like *White Collar Brawlers* and other remediated entertainments, not in the traditional way of, say, a Tyler Durden from *Fight Club*). In fact, that he is not buff and/or trim is supposed to serve as further evidence of his sincerity, his approach-ability, his 'realness.' Anyway, to spend so many hours at the gym would mean the other guy is missing out on the important stuff, playing *Madden NFL* with his friends, taking his kids to Tae Kwon Do, cleaning the house so that his working wife can put her feet up at the end of a hard day, laboring at work and in the do-mestic space to keep the new (yet fading) middle-class dream in abundance. The other guy's body, ostensibly, has to come second. Yet, he is prone to spending a bit more for a nice moisturizer, so that he can shave his chest and genitals. That way, his partner (who is also shaved) feels that things are equal in the bedroom and out. His hair might be mildly styled, but not primped—cut so that he could be taken seriously at the work dinner he attends before heading out to the local club to catch a rock show by a band with a propulsive female lead singer and a drummer who eschews solos and fancy equipment.

For certain, the other guy is wired. He follows Twitter, but doesn't tweet much (that would be too celebratory). He uses an iPhone, but if he still has a Blackberry, it's out of loyalty to his other friends that still use one. His Face-book page is full of family pictures where he is featured alongside others, never in center frame. His history is straightforward, with exactly two quirky details, as is his friend list (lots of 'close' friends, but even more 'friends'). He really seems to like most everything—in fact the 'like' button is central to his dig-ital and analog psychology. Some would even call him a pushover; instead of the standard 'fight' or 'flight' impulses often relegated to a regressive, ma-cho masculinity, he consistently relies on a third 'f'—'fix.' This fixing impulse is definitive of the other guy, it represents his acknowledgment of a central dialectic at work within him: the assumed position of criticism and 'father knows best' born out of the homogenous, entitled, masculine monolith of the patriarchy, and the empathic, nurturing, constructive side of the new male as product of feminism, the culture wars and pop psychology. However, the other guy seems to fundamentally know that the urge to 'fix' is one that is heavily criticized by his partners, particularly women. A well-worn trope of the last decade in pop culture, this situation features the female admonishing her male partner to 'just listen' to her feelings, instead of the more stereotypical, male impulse to 'fix the problem.' In a heavily viewed YouTube short entitled, "It's Not About the Nail!" a mid-thirties, attractive white couple are engaged in a conversation, with the woman describing at length the pain and constant pressure she feels in her head, day in and day out. He responds, "You do have a nail in your head." We then see that she does indeed have a nail sticking out of her forehead. She responds, "It's not about the nail!" This short elucidates not only who the other guy is, but what he is struggling with, as well as how he is framed and represented in the media (and this same argument is played out in countless films, TV shows and commercials).

What is notable about these scenarios is that we—the external viewer, reader, audience—are supposed to implicitly understand something about men in general here—that they would never have this level of miscommunication amongst *themselves*, as men all 'want the same things' and inherently 'get' each other. This, of course, is completely incorrect. Men are crushingly competitive with each other, often cruel in their application and maintenance of masculine hierarchies, and violent toward difference and alterity. So, this dubious argument will frame my arguments in this book, particularly that the other guy is inhabiting a type of liminal gender space, a transitional moment where more is expected of men, emotionally, psychologically, socially and physically, and how the other guy (by dealing with new requirements—like listening) struggles to find a place in the alpha/beta/omega hierarchy of men while acknowledging and respecting their partners as different, yet knowable, and presumably, equal. And so a central component of my argument is that the other guy is an approach as well as a person, a tactic in the face of a changing social, economic and ideological landscape that enables the other guy to find a workable spot on the stereotypical gamut strung between traditional 'masculinity' and 'femininity.' I argue that other guy masculinity is fundamentally heuristic, as opposed to the intensely fixed monoliths of the patriarchy (as well as the very real process of opposition) that are often expressed as being non-dialectical—outside the realm of opposites, where femininity is instead seen not as an opposite but as a lesser state (endless becoming and not being), so that men themselves are material extensions of Authority, the patriarchy as fiat. The other guy is, then, difference within white masculinity itself, which means that he has already begun the process of decoupling with the structures of power—but not without regret, of course. As I have mentioned, a fundamental and pervasive melancholy exists in other guyness, expressed in his mild and occasional apathy, as well as his comportment and carriage. His body is still useful, but it can't quite measure up. Even Disney has gotten the picture with the loping and lackadaisical other guy Kristoff in the mega-hit animated movie *Frozen* (2013). As the song from the film goes, "He's a Bit of a Fixer-Upper," a guy who would rather hang out with his buddy (and pet) reindeer, Sven, than with other men or women. But, in the end, he is cajoled into helping the Princess foil the plans of Hans, a Machiavellian and cruel alpha male. Here, the plot revolves around the choices of the women, with the men occupying secondary roles, a heteronormative afterthought as opposed to a defining ideological message.

The Game Plan

Front and center in the new gender logics is the other guy's body on display, often ridiculed for not acquiescing to the more familiar mythopoetics of the macho, muscle-bound hunks seen on screens since the rise of the New Hollywood cinema and the action blockbuster. Additionally, the discipline of masculinities studies has matured alongside these bodily displays, as has the inclusion of theories of male representations on screen in film studies. Chapter 1 theorizes these connected methodologies and approaches together as a means of elucidating the genesis of the other guy, as well as more ubiquitous, contemporary discourse surrounding men and masculinity. Historically, the other guy is also certainly a product of the dissemination and dilution of masculine types that has resulted from the digital media revolution—whether that is through male self-help websites, streaming video of *Jackass*-style pranks, online videogame banter, or the rise of the power-geek (a Steve Jobs-style über-nerd with a god complex and coding skills). Accompanying this digital dispersal, sharing and enunciation is the rise of indie films in the U.S., particularly the mumblecore genre (covered in Chapter 2), which consistently feature representations of the other guy, but which are also *produced* by other guys, slacker hipsters like Mark Duplass. Additionally, the films of Judd Apatow offer glimpses of the anxieties and desires of the other guy, particularly in relation to further masculine types and their masculine tactics. Of particular importance here is the work of Stella Bruzzi, specifically her reworking of the concept "men's cinema" and "masculinity in film studies." Not only does the figuration of the other guy break with standard filmic modes of masculine representation, but the films themselves (brom-coms, for instance) challenge notions of genre and form.[3] In Chapter 3, I analyze other guys on TV, particularly in sitcoms, a well-worn environment where the more traditional elements in television production can attack new modes of being and identity, while superficially giving voice to emergent types and forms (like the reality-TV format of *Modern Family*, for example). Finally, in Chapter 4, I examine the other guy's body a bit more closely in a variety of settings, from popular music to reality TV, advertising to popular psychology. Understanding the shifts in male power and position over the past decade involves unpacking assumptions about the male body, particularly in relation to concepts like 'metrosexual' (the recent, urban, chic masculinity) or 'manscaping' (upkeep and pampering of the male body). While the popular press, advertising and consumption patterns have changed for males, what is habitually touted as a new male attitude or identity is often a set of consumer choices, a branding exercise and/or demographic loci. Indeed, many men have changed the way that they think of their bodies, and the way their bodies are thought of, yet much of these changes are versions of the oppressive and shallow beauty standard forced on women, so that the other guy often seems befuddled and apathetic toward the new standards. This highlights the dangers in theorizing contemporary masculinities; if the subject is white and middle-class, the discussion can so easily turn toward a 'crisis' in masculinity (akin to the Christian persecution fantasies that frequent Fox News) that may obfuscate the real anxieties and issues facing these men. I end the chapter with the Penny Arcade 'dickwolves' controversy, an example of the majority-as-victim trope played out online in a war of words that highlights more general notions of free speech, body politics, rape culture and how digital masculinity might slowly be learning that their victim trope is both fruitless and counter-productive.

This leads me to a central concept that enshrouds and defines the other guy—*synaesthetic masculinity*—a mélange of synesthesia and aesthetics. It's a state of being and an identity position devised from the constant, eliding media phantasmagoria that encircles modern boys and men. From beauty products to self-help books, films, TV and videogames, the other guy is a particularly reactive identity, a response to the myriad social, cultural and economic changes he (and his family, friends, partners, co-workers) faces daily. The sheer volume and regularity of the information, images and products can lead to crossed wires, a 'synaesthetic' identity where notions of what previously constituted 'acceptable male behavior' are cued by competing messages, resulting in a jumbled male aesthetic, behavior and mode of identification. Do I shave my chest now, or is hair back in? Am I working on my listening skills this week, or on my Instagram portfolio? Am I sincerely disgusted with Arnold Schwarzenegger's new film, or do I enjoy it ironically? Is it ok to make fun of my child's gluten allergy with my male friends, even if my wife and I already make fun of it at home? This swirling morass triggers the other guy's melancholia, his sense of confused bemusement, like so many of the characters Paul Rudd portrays in TV, film and on the web. Like the end of the Cold War and the geopolitical instability that followed, the other guy's cold war conflict—his long, slow-burn resentment and distrust of women, men, and himself has been replaced with a new set of instabilities, contingencies and competing interests. The long and fabled battle within men still persists, but it's been drawn outward so that the conflicts are spoken, shared and blogged about.

In the work of Mikhail Bakhtin, particularly his unfinished early essay "Toward a Philosophy of the Act," the author sets forth his structural schematic for the human psyche, identity formation as a product of the continuum between the self and others. In a sense, this is a rejection of Kantian and Cartesian philosophies of the mind and the self, as well as an early form of his later dialogical schema, further pursued in his works on literature and language. In the essay, he posits three intertwined and composite psychic structures: "I-for-myself," "I-for-the-other," and "other-for-me." These correspond loosely to more general divisions between subjects and objects, as well as interiority and exteriority. What is key here is Bakhtin's stance that "I-for-myself" is an untenable mode of identity, in that it constantly folds back on itself and fails to acknowledge the external as crucial in subject formation, hence the importance of "I-for-the-other" as a mediating force. The balance between the two results in a composite and equalized understanding of the self, predicated on one's knowledge of how others see the self. Similarly, "other-for-me" operates through others' incorporation of how one sees them, in their own notion of self.[4] Thus, identity is a continuum that is shared and maintained by all. In contemplating the value of the other guy as a transitional form of masculinity, I would like to use Bakhtin's schematic to highlight the importance of empathy in identity formation, and argue that the other guy is symptomatic of a masculinity that recognizes that "I-for-the-other" and "other-for-me" are not only sustainable, valuable aspects of the self, but that they aren't necessarily at odds with masculinity itself. In this sense, the other guy is perhaps not engaged in the more traditional sciamachy that seems to plague modern masculinities, suppressed struggles that result in the familiar self-aggrandizing, proving and overcompensating of macho maleness.

Notes

1. Kaja Silverman, *Male Subjectivity at the Margins* (London: Routledge, 1992), p. 52.
2. *The Onion*, "Area Man Unsure If He's Male-Bonding or Being Bullied," Sept 19, 2013, retrieved from theonion.com.

3. Stella Bruzzi, *Men's Cinema: Masculinity and Mise en Scène in Hollywood*. Edinburgh: Edinburgh U. Press, 2013.

4. Gary Morrison and Caryl Emmerson, *Mikhail Bakhtin: Creation of a Prosaics*. Stanford, CA: Stanford U. Press, 1990. *The Dialogic Imagination: Four Essays by Mikhail Bakhtin*. Ed. Michael Holquist. Trans. Caryl Emerson and Michael Holquist. Austin: U. of Texas Press, 1982.

· 1 ·

IT'S NOT YOU, IT'S ME

I've seen the emergence of your kind like an infection,
all these effete, over-articulate man-boys who never learned to
toughen up. Don't be one of them. Go work with your hands
Build something. Punch someone in the face.
Actress Alison Janney in the film Liberal Arts (2012)

In the 2009 film *I Love You, Man*, nice guy Paul Rudd plays other guy Peter Klaven, a Los Angeles realtor who is on a search for the best man for his wedding. The trouble is, he doesn't have any male friends and has always had difficulty connecting with guys. As his gay brother states (played by Andy Samberg), "Peter has always been a girlfriend guy. He put all his focus and energy in his relationships and his dude friends just fell by the wayside." To remedy this, Peter's fiancée and family attempt to set him up on a series of 'mandates' (non-sexual dates with other straight men), most of which end up as awkward as bad dates in rom-coms often do. However this film turns this scenario on its head by playing with the usual heterosexual hijinks that populate the genre. Peter is, as it turns out, an other guy—he frequents a fencing gym, is a mediocre real estate agent, wears unfussy clothes and has a hard time understanding male rules and roles, and is particularly flummoxed by 'guy speak,' the heterosexual male dialect made up of insults, 'smack-talk,' and homophobic and sexist jokes.

He gets along with women and is a 'serial monogamist.' In fact, he 'gets' women, to the point that it alienates other males around him. He can't quite get the hang of the 'guy code,' an unwritten series of rules and regulations that men use to police each other, turning women into part enemy/part exotic Other, and gay men into untrustworthy sexual predators (of straight men). To men who subscribe to the guy code, gay men have rejected the 'natural' course of gender relations and heteronormative functionality. And yet, it is Peter who is cast as the glitch when his wife's female friend says, "A guy without friends can be really clingy," something Peter overhears on his way into the living room with root beer floats for the women over at their house for 'ladies night,' intimating that these women have bought into the guy code as well (or, too often, have little choice in the matter). "I gotta get some fucking friends," Peter says to himself. Directives abound in the film. At one point his brother gives him advice on mandates: "…casual lunch, after work drinks. No dinner and no movies." And, so after several failed mandates, Peter serendipitously meets the male partner with whom he can have a bromance (a non-sexual, close, male friendship), Sydney Fife, played by the mildly eccentric Jason Segal. Sydney is a fascinating blend of new male characteristics: while he retains some of the hallmarks of what R.W. Connell has identified as hegemonic (straight, white, middle-class) masculinity, he is also articulate, a free spirit, emotionally open, a womanizer, and a kind of guru about human nature, behavior, body language and desire. He drives a scooter (instead of, say, a muscle car), lives in a beach bungalow, owns a puggle (a cross between a pug and a beagle), wears skinny scarves, long sweaters and Ugg boots (in a subtle ode to young women's fashion at the time), plays the guitar, and has built a 'man cave' behind his bungalow (a men-only space, filled with TVs, musical instruments, toys, a beer fridge and a masturbation station). "I'm a man, Peter," Sydney says, "I've got an ocean of testosterone flowing through my veins. Society tells us to act civilized, but sometimes you gotta let it out." And while Sydney does engage in sexist and other obnoxious behaviors, one senses that at least he *sees himself* as a new male—a man that understands his emotions, desires and skills, while engaging in activities clearly quoting the Hugh Hefner bachelor-playboy of the 1950s and '60s.[1]

There are, of course, narrative requirements at work here—if Sydney didn't retain some of the Boomer and/or hipster masculine traits and predilections, Peter wouldn't have a subjectivity and persona to mimic (and eventually partially reject). Also, the film was originally written in the late 1990s, and so it is reasonable to assert that some of Sydney's traits are at odds with his more 'progressive' male traits because of the changes in masculinity during the 2000s (*Queer Eye for the Straight Guy*, the Judd Apatow films, the rise of the Paul Rudd brand and style). Additionally, the director, John Hamburg, moved from New York to Los Angeles in the mid 2000s and noticed that, as a middle-aged male, it had become harder to find male friends, and that Los Angeles itself, with its automobile-insularity and endless sprawl, created additional hurdles.[2] Considering that masculinities across the country are subject to local and quotidian cultural and economic factors, Hamburg's dilemma does feel distinctly West Coast (and add to this the fact that many of the new male/other guy films are shot in L.A.). So, while there are wide discrepancies between Peter and Sydney (coincidental with the parts that Rudd and Segal seem to repetitively play in film and TV) as characters, both fall somewhere on the other guy spectrum. The other guy is the new white, middle-class male who is neither too attractive or too ugly, neither successful or not, an outgrowth of the Beta male that has developed out of the economic, cultural and historical exigencies of the male movement of the 1990s, the digital revolution and .com boom and bust of the early 2000s, the anxiety and reactionary politics of the Bush administration, and the global recession beginning in 2008. What is so valuable about *I Love You, Man* is its constant push and pull between white male victimization and optimistic cheerleading for these two characters, both flawed men who are giving it their best shot in a rapidly changing world, one where white masculinity is on the descent. In this sense, both of these characters represent a real-world struggle between the more conservative, traditional masculinity of post-WWII America and the rise of the progressive, utopic male, trying to make sense of women and the LGBTT community, along with, and in reaction to, his own body and desires. As Sydney says to Peter during one of his pep talks, "You have all the skills in the world, but you have no confidence. Now, sac up, man," as he reaches for and taps Peter's testicles, an action that disavows the homoerotic by doubling-down on the homosocial, an unspoken barrier broken in service of the powerful urge to bond 'bromantically.'

In this chapter, it's my aim to theorize the other guy in relation to selected works in two complimentary areas, film studies and masculinities studies, in order to draw attention to a central aspect of the other guy: the other guy as a form of *synaesthetic masculinity*, a concept introduced earlier. To reiterate, synaesthetic masculinity is an identity position that is founded on the crossed and confusing sensory information the other guy receives in the form of aesthetic rules and trends, film and TV, videogames, and postmodern life in general. In this sense, the other guy is answering the consumerist hail, albeit in a way that doesn't always seem logical. The other guy is certainly on display in film and on TV (and through other media), but the display is complicated by his less-than-macho physique, his acquiescence to female criticism and confusion over the 'guy code,' the set of rules and conventions that men must follow in order to 'measure up,' while also serving as a protocol that excludes female participation. In essence, part of the pleasure of watching the other guy is to watch him squirm, attempting to navigate the twin minefields of modern female (if not feminist) expectation and contemporary masculine crisis and sequestration. Synesthesia, where, for instance, a sound can register as a color in the perceptive process, is an apt diagnosis here, for the other guy's life is a juggling act, and part of what makes the other guy so often a sympathetic, comic figure (as opposed to Woody Allen's anxiety-ridden comic angst, or Dennis Leary's vitriolic, Boston tough-guy shtick) is his confused (mis)application of the new rules, and the aesthetic jumble that results (clothing, hair and comportment, but also phraseology, manners and style). Paul Rudd's flubbing of Jason Segal's cool-speak in *I Love You, Man* comes to mind ("lateress on the meningies"—or something like that—instead of "see you later, man"). The other guy often functions as comic foil or fool, as much a part of the comedic narrative of masculinity as he is a character within those narratives. This is mirrored in the kind of snark and smart-ass attitude that is so prevalent amongst other guy bloggers, tweeters and netizens—a practiced attitude that emphasizes cool over content as a means of erasing the lack of improvisational skill that ended in guy-time disaster at the bar last night. In many ways, this defensive, comic stance is a direct result of the ubiquity of the 'guy code' and is a type of response to the excesses of what Michael Kimmel calls "Guyland." In his engrossing study of young men (ages 16–26) across America, Kimmel identifies key features of this time and space:

> Guyland is the world in which young men live. It is both a stage of life, a liminal undefined time span between adolescence and adulthood that can often stretch for a decade or more, and a place, or, rather, a bunch of places where guys gather to be guys with each other, unhassled by the demands of parents, girlfriends, jobs, kids, and the other nuisances of adult life. In this topsy-turvy, Peter-Pan mindset, young men shirk the responsibilities of adulthood and remain fixated on the trappings of boyhood, while the boys they still are struggle heroically to prove that they are real men despite all the evidence to the contrary.[3]

Kimmel's emphasis on 'shirking' and 'proving' is key; these dudes are caught between the dual impulses of avoiding *while* corroborating their masculinity. And Hollywood constantly targets them as consumers, as does the videogame industry and electronics and sports markets. So, between the playtime of videogames (boyhood and regression) and the violent and sexist action films and TV shows tailor-made for them (machismo and verification), as well as in the pages of *Maxim*, hip-hop music and sports, Guyland guys, according to Kimmel's research, are systematically avoiding maturity and turning into the kind of men that are neither progressive nor productive. However, during the same decade that Kimmel was researching and writing the book, the other guy started to slowly appear in the same films and TV shows aimed at these men. Arguably, this 'stuff' was also aimed at men who had extended this immaturity into their 30s, and/or are evincing regret and frisson at leaving Guyland behind. So, in this sense, the other guy is an *inter-mediatic identity*, one formed on screens, as much as it is in the real world, by real guys (hence 'synaesthetic'). For more often than not, other guys quote their favorite films and TV and a means of communication and indexical erudition, as do the representations of the other guy on screen, in an eliding and sinuous acknowledgment of post-modern ironic detachment and euphoric mediatic-identity formation.

The Scene and the Screen

The first signs of the other guy appeared in the 2000s, namely in a series of films, television shows and advertisements that featured heterosexual families where the father was the primary breadwinner, but the mother also worked, often outside the home. The typical situation features a family 'figuring it out,' confused by the new gender order, yet embracing the new changes they must face. At the core of this is the rise of women in the workplace and how this played out in the public and the domestic. While men certainly did and continue to hold the majority of the positions of power at work, the traditional concept of fathers and husbands (and workers) was, in a sense, under attack. Middle class homes now featured a new sort of complexity—often referred to as 'juggling'—who picks the kids of up from school, who takes them to sports practice, and who makes dinner were suddenly up for grabs, with the children often represented as lost in the shuffle or, in the least, confused as to who is supposed to do what. Several major economic and social trends show the extent of these changes. U.S. male labor-force participation has been in a steady decline while female labor participation has steadily risen in the past four decades. "Women are less likely than they were in the past to leave a job and drop out of the labor force to raise a family, take care of aging parents or family members, or for other reasons," while the likelihood of men quitting and not looking for work has increased.[4] Factors for these changes include U.S. men receiving less substantial work skills (women's enrollment in college has outpaced men's[5]), lower or stagnating wages for men, as well as globalization, less powerful labor unions, the speed of technological change, and changes in the workplace that make it easier for mothers to work.[6] Additionally, U.S. women ages 18–34 now, "…surpass young men in the importance they place on having a high-paying career or profession."[7] And finally, amongst men and women in 22 nations surveyed by the Pew Research Center's Global Attitudes Report conducted in 2010,

> …solid majorities express support for gender equality and agree that women should be able to work outside the home. Most also find a marriage in which both spouses share financial and household responsibilities to be more satisfying than one in which the husband provides for the family and the wife takes care of the home and children.[8]

It is highly possible that life in a postindustrial economy is better suited to women, and that men and the masculine hegemony is failing to adjust to the requirements of a communications/service-based economies. This shift would necessarily not be biologically based—I argue throughout this book that it is a matter of acculturated social roles, identity adaptability and economic pragmatism. French sociologist Pierre Bourdieu documented this in his fascinating 2008 book *The Bachelor's Ball*, an analysis of changing gender roles and socio-economic shift in the French region of Béarn, where the men remained tied to land that no longer produced, while the women left for professional jobs in the cities. While women appear to be more adept at identifying and shifting toward the dominant mode of production, men seem to rely on traditional labor modes and masculine privilege.[9]

The discourse around these economic and social shifts is where we find the genesis of the other guy. Like women juggling work and family, the personal and the public, men too had to develop a performance of equity, balance and evolution. Not only is the other guy supposed to listen, he is supposed to cry, particularly after the psychotherapy sessions, whether formally on the couch, or informally with his buddies at the bar. The other guy and his ilk are, of course, only one small subset of the global hegemonic masculinity machine, but they are important historically, as with their appearance, something sinister was also afoot. By agreeing to embrace the new masculinity, these men were (and are) performing a kind of masculinity where they are able to 'have it all'—be the 'man' they were raised to be by their fathers and friends, but also be the kind of partner that women had come to expect, largely through examples offered by the popular media. While the other guy does seem to be adapting, and adaptable, he still inhabits a tricky victimized position—so that he can fall back on his secondary status as 'other' to the more macho, alpha male, and thus explain away why he has 'chosen' to be the nice guy. In a delicate and ornately embellished performance, the other guy still operates as the white, heterosexual male suffering at the hands of women's movements and other forms of Western alterity, while attempting to traverse the changing economic and social landscape as a man that seeks to also defy traditional gender expectations. In order to trace the genesis of the other guy, I would like to turn back to early film theory on masculinity in order to tease out the interests and preoccupations of the theorists as well as the subjects and objects on display, later moving to a more complete discussion of changes within the study of masculinities itself. By doing so, the mediatic origins of synaesthetic masculinity will be uncovered and intertwined with the process of identification, categorization and theorization undertaken by masculinities studies.

A common starting point for the study of gender and cinema (and visual culture, in general) is Laura Mulvey's seminal essay, "Visual Pleasure and Narrative Cinema," first published in *Screen* in 1975. This highly influential essay laid bare the psychic underpinnings of cinema and its inherently patriarchal visual structuring. Important concepts such as the Male Gaze and scopophilia continue to provide useful purchase in film theory, as well as media theory in general. At the core of Mulvey's theory is visual power—the female body as 'looked-at' with the male body doing the looking, and the camera (and presumably, the male director looking through the camera onto both bodies, as well as the audience assuming both of these male visual positions). This not only demarcated masculinity as subject and female as object, but revealed that cinema itself is bound up in the politics of power played out in the Real. What is telling about Mulvey's work and the time period in which it was written, is that men and masculinity itself was largely theorized as occupying one side of the gendered equation, so that a discursive either/or infused conceptions of masculinity on screen, as well as in the mode of production itself. This can be extended to the male body as well. Yet, particularly in contemporary cinema, the male body has become increasingly fluid and unstable, so that he may occupy multiple positions, often simultaneously. Men talk, chat, and whine onscreen now, sometimes at painful lengths. They cry, they break down, and then they admit defeat. And then talk about it some more. In Mulvey's readings, men were assumed to inhabit a solitary (and often solipsistic) subjectivity, stern and stoic, whereas in later decades, men on screen were showing signs of aging, wear and tear, anxiety and self-doubt. The 1996 film *Swingers* serves as a prime example of conflicted masculinity exploring itself through self-reflexive critique and conversation, in a particularly other-guy fashion.

Further early studies on gender in film echo Mulvey's astute readings, while at the same time making room for fluidity in masculine representation. In "Masculinity as Spectacle: Reflections on Men and Mainstream Cinema," Steve Neale (writing in 1983) writes, "It is thus very rare to find analyses that seek to specify in detail, in relation to particular films or groups of films, how heterosexual masculinity is inscribed and the mechanisms, pressures, and contradictions that inscription may involve."[10] Here, Neale is specifically referring to how heterosexual masculinity appears as a "structural norm in relation to both images of women and gay men." He continues with an adept reading of numerous films with an eye toward identification, voyeuristic looking and fetishistic looking, arguing that where Mulvey uses these figurations in relation to women, they should also be utilized in the analysis of screened men. What is telling here is that Neale is making a point in relation to Mulvey's essay, and by extension, offering a response to feminist film theory. Whereas the operant logic at the time of his writing was to focus on monolithic, or, again, "hegemonic masculinity," focusing on men as not only part of the power discourse, but also as an unlikely ally in the unmaking of patriarchical power, was not yet up for grabs. This is, as I will show, a product of the evolution of film theory, but also of the evolution of masculinities as a discipline, or put another way, men as objects of study who don't simply occupy positions of power, but bring that power into question by the performativity of that power, an acknowledgment of the transitive and constructed nature of representational power.

I would argue that the three psychic functions set forth by Mulvey—identification, voyeuristic looking and fetishistic looking—still hold great value, but have shifted in their meanings, as the heterosexual men on screen have shifted in their meaning-making. Returning to Neale, he discusses John Ellis's book *Visible Fictions*, paying particular attention to narcissism and its relation to cinematic identification:

> In looking specifically at masculinity in this context, I want to examine the process
> of narcissistic identification in more detail. Inasmuch as films *do* [author's emphasis]
> involve gender identification, and inasmuch as current ideologies of masculinity involve
> so centrally notions and attitudes to do with aggression, power, and control, it seems to
> me that narcissism and narcissistic identification may be especially significant.[11]

Certainly with the rise of reality TV and the self-made, conflict-driven, accidental star (any of the cast from *Jersey Shore*), narcissism as discourse in itself is significant, and I will continue to return to it throughout the book, as it is a defining, albeit repressed, feature of the other guy. However, for Neale, the films of Anthony Mann reveal a male body that is on screen to "exist"—to move, act, fuck—and the pleasure of this existence is derived from a repressed homosexual voyeurism. Think here of 'The Man with No Name' as played by Clint Eastwood in the Sergio Leone spaghetti Westerns. We watch him ride alone, walk alone, shoot alone—through various environments and scenarios, as if he is a living statue—a tall, lean avatar for our collective wishes to transcend the quotidian. Yet, this voyeurism is inherently contradictory; it itself cannot bear the gaze of another male, nor can the spectator eroticize the screened body for fear of self-retaliation or being 'found out.' At the core of narcissism is the need to look at oneself, after all, as well as being looked at by others, and here is where the difference between narcissism and narcissistic identification plays out. Men both desire to be looked at and desire to look, yet the precarious nature of heterosexuality precludes a male's ability to look at another male body erotically, *unless* that body can be consumed by identification and subsumed into their own narcissism. 'I bet he and I would be friends—he seems just like me.' And so this is played out in various structures, characterizations and ideological modes. Needless to say, in Mulvey's early work, the Western is the genre where this is staged *ne plus ultra*.

Neale continues his discussion of narcissism by highlighting another central conflict within screenic masculine narcissism, "It is the contradiction between narcissism and the law, between an image of narcissistic authority on the one hand and an image of social authority on the other."[12] Particularly important to this study—whether to join the social order or not—this conflict enunciates and itself desires a narrative function. At some point, men on screen are expected to act, to make a choice and join the world of men and women (and all others), or continue to exist solely in the world of men. In my previous book, *Die Tryin: Masculinity, Videogames, Culture*, I trace this regressive tendency—what I term "boyhood"—in males subsumed by digital culture, where the male can eschew his responsibilities and narcissistically continue to play his games, on screen and out in the world. This narcissistic process of identification features prominently in the narratives of the other-guy films, particularly in the films starring Paul Rudd (more fully explored in Chapter 2). What I want to focus on here is that, for cinema and masculinity studies in the 1980s, a complex functional map of masculine performance and behavior was already well under way, albeit much of it was still in response to feminism and the rise of women's movements. So, let's mark narcissistic identification as a central feature (both historically and theoretically) on the male body. And it is here that I want to introduce an imagistic and physical trope that I encourage the reader to play with throughout this book, an other guy's body that will function as a type of 'pin-the-tail-on-the-donkey' exercise (imagine one that suits you). For narcissistic identification, I would like you to place it on the other guy's dick. It can be a tag, a sticker, a pushpin, a Magic Marker 'x'—whatever turns you on (or off). I encourage the reader to buy a poster of your most or least favorite dude, and post it on a wall. This can serve as a readerly activity that pokes a whole in an idea, marks off territory, celebrates a physicality, destabilizes a piece of flesh, or objectifies and debases. Narcissistic identification and the dick certainly seem linked in my mind, where the penis and the phallus in a constant representative dance mark the masculine interpellation by the law, by women and by other men. I use the term dick to dredge up the word as it is used by so many heterosexual and gay men. "Don't be a dick." "You're a dick." "That was dickish." These admonitions serve as many things: a homophobic denial of another man's penis (and therefore his sexuality, and therefore any homoerotics between the two or the group), a subtle critique of men who only 'think with their dicks,' a constant reminder of the presence of the male body as the definitive source of men's power.

Returning to Neale, voyeuristic looking (the first of Mulvey's two visual structures), "is marked by the extent to which there is a distance between the spectator and spectacle, a gulf between the seer and the seen. This structure is one which allows the spectator a degree of power over what is seen."[13] This position of power is fraught with male castration anxieties and is therefore imbued with sado-masochistic fantasies, so that the male doing the looking is simultaneously enacting a violence toward what is seen (primarily a woman), while avoiding the painful realization of losing his bodily site of power (his penis). Neale extends his critique to several genres (the Western, war films and gangster movies) in order to tease out the centrality of the struggle, the duel, the battle. If, as Neale points out, the male body is constantly on display during these conflicts (in order to enact a sado-masochistic fantasy), the male bodies themselves are a site of voyeuristic pleasure. Think here of the Schwarzenegger or Stallone films of the 1980s, where the rippling muscles, shirtless torsos and blood-stained skin are constantly on display (and often penetrated), presumably for male, as well as female, pleasure.[14] While this situation and these struggles on screen continue to unfold, what we see most often in contemporary Hollywood cinema is the male body on display either as nostalgic marker of the excesses of Reagan-era machismo (*The Expendables* series, where the action heroes of yesterday return to again prove their mettle), or the beyond-the-body anthropomorphisms as seen in the *Transformers* series, in *Real Steel* (2011; a fighting robot-avatar that re-bonds a father and son), or in the up-the-ante globalized invasion narrative of *Battleship* (2012) or *Pacific Rim* (2013). So, whereas voyeuristic looking now includes both the female body and the male body, so too have the sado-masochistic function and the castration anxieties—these pleasures and annulments have been displaced on the technologies of extension brought on by digitization, while still containing remnants and palimpsests of the Real-Man technologies of the industrial age. Strangely, an answer to this seemingly endless cacophony of masculinized bodies, battles and weaponry is the other guy—the dude with the 'normal' body, the one who eschews the gym, has gained some weight and is staring middle age in the face, albeit rarely straight in the eyes. A key factor in this transition to a male figure that looks a bit more like the rest of us (albeit, so many of the other guys are white) is the buddy film of the 1980s and '90s. But, let us first attend to the second of Mulvey's visual structures, scopophilic fetishism.

Mulvey writes, "The beauty of the woman as object and screen space coalesce; she is no longer the bearer of guilt but a perfect product, whose body, stylized and fragmented by close-ups, is the content of the film and the direct recipient of the spectator's look."[15] Think here of the workout scene from *Flashdance* (1983), a scene that functions as a music video as much as a girl-bonding scene, where the women (in their tight-fitting, glistening and revealing workout clothes) are fragmented into the distinct erotic-dancer components: buttocks, breasts and head. Neale analyzes this passage and finds that while this is true for the films that Mulvey uses in her analysis in regards to women: "We are not offered the spectacle of male bodies, but bodies unmarked as objects of erotic display. …We see male bodies stylized and fragmented by close-ups, but our look is not direct, it is heavily mediated by the looks of the characters involved."[16] Neale does find exceptions. Rock Hudson in Douglas Sirk's melodramas is a particularly interesting counter-example, yet, as he argues, Hudson's body is distinctly feminized, and therefore 'safe' to gaze at, "An indication of the strength of those conventions which dictate that only women can function as the objects of an explicitly erotic gaze."[17] And, while Neale agrees with Mulvey in that the spectator in Hollywood cinema is a fundamentally male subject, there exist cracks and fissures not only in the way that we look (as men), but in the figurations and bodies on screen at which we gaze. One obvious example is the gay male body (think of the wonderfully complicated role Dennis Quaid plays in Todd Haynes' Sirkian deconstruction, *Far From Heaven* [2002]). Another is the conflagrated masculinity that arises out of the buddy film. This, in turn, sets the stage for the entrance of the other guy at the outset of the 21st century.

I would like again to reach back to an important essay from the past in order to continue to trace the threads of how men are represented on screen today, namely through Cynthia J. Fuchs' essay, "The Buddy Politic."[18] In the essay, Fuchs inspects the cinematic male bond portrayed in a variety of films from the action genre during the 1980s. Fuchs writes,

> …the problem of male self-identity is exacerbated by its apparent resolution. For this conspicuous discharge situates the male couple between the representational poles of homoeroticism and homophobia, in love with their self-displays and at odds with their implications. Caught inside conventions of 'male-bonding' and outside racist, heterosexual norms, the buddy politic can only implode.[19]

She finds that these films, and the male relationships within them, mark historical transitions in masculinities, from the Vietnam War to the Gulf War and beyond. Additionally, these films are representative of U.S. presidential administrations and their responses to an ever-globalized capitalist system, and the ideological shifts and inconsistencies apparent in these administrations' policies. Key to these films is the manner in which the 'buddy relationship' is played out and how homophobia is disavowed while the homosocial bond grows rife with contradiction and promise. In a rather brilliant reading of the first two *Lethal Weapon* films (1987, 1989), Fuchs finds that the manner in which Mel Gibson's young, lithe, sinuously muscled and potentially lethal body is contrasted with Danny Glover's older, weary, black body. "Where the borderline psychotic Riggs [Gibson] would kill himself, Murtaugh (Glover) is concerned with self-preservation." Here, Fuchs is focused on how each character sees themselves as a former soldier (in the Vietnam War), and subsequently, how each has dealt with trauma. Throughout the films, Riggs' body is on constant display—it is taut, white, conditioned and psychologically broken, but it always 'wins' in the end. Murtaugh's body, however, is shown as always on the edge of retirement, his time as a soldier having been left behind in favor of family and career—"I'm too old for this shit." His body, similarly, is rarely on display—he wears a suit and tie, and carries a revolver (as opposed to Riggs' semi-automatic pistol), a gun that, as Riggs comments, is something that, "a lot of old-timers like." These two men, and their bodies, represent the two opposing forces of the greatest generation and the transitional generation of masculinity, with Murtaugh as a stand-in for tradition, solidity, family and country. Riggs, on the other hand, is fighting his battles on the inside as well as the outside—he clearly suffers from PTSD (a harbinger of so many men and women returning from the wars in Iraq and Afghanistan), and functions as a stand-in for white masculinity under attack, anxious about the women's movement, the rise of the queer rights and ethnic groups previously considered outside the realm of 'true' America. Yet these men have each other's back, so to speak. They watch each other's ass. In the final scene of *Lethal Weapon 2*, Riggs, penetrated by bullets, beaten and possibly dying, lies in the arms of Murtaugh, who gently holds him, telling him to "hold on." Riggs, appearing at the edge of death, after a long pause, answers, "Give us a kiss," a simultaneous acknowledgment of their bond and disavowal of the homoerotics that are so often forged in heat of battle, in the peculiar space of action, conflict and death. And, as Fuchs writes, "If impending death allows these exaggerated images of male-on-male contact, such images also link violence and sexuality, to the point that women are simply ejected from the script."[20] But, what of the humor used by Riggs, in the throes of a death spasm, 'knock-knock-knocking on heaven's door'? As spectators, are we in on the joke? Or is the joke on us? I focus on this scene because, as we will see, humor is a central mechanism of disavowal for the other guy, an adaptation to the above-mentioned wave of 'otherness' faced by the white male at the end of the 20th century. I want to again emphasize that Fuchs' reading of these films shows, like Neale, a rising tide of interest in male bodies and minds on screen during the 1980s and '90s, and in particular, how schematics of visual power must attend to the male body and how it is represented as a complex and dynamic sexual locus. As Barry Keith Grant writes in his 2011 study of masculinity within genre films, *Shadows of Doubt*, "Critics now understand that while representations of masculinity may have been the center from which Others were defined, it was not simply one uncontested construction of masculinity that was at play in movies."[21]

In Stella Bruzzi's probing and groundbreaking book, *Men's Cinema: Masculinity and Mise en Scène in Hollywood*, the author seeks to reformulate how men in cinema are theorized, as well as what constitutes a "men's cinema." Bruzzi, after covering the centrality of the body in Mulvey's early work (as well as the ramifications for a great deal of film theory, particularly the overwhelming adherence (for a time) to feminist film theory as a means of understanding masculinity on screen, in the theater seats and behind the camera), finds that Neale's approach hems too closely to Mulvey's schematic, and that, "Ultimately, masculinity is stopped from descending into 'pure spectacle' by the acceptance of Mulvey's psychodynamic paradigm, a paradigm that is here reiterated at the expense of any further discussion of style and aesthetics as generators of meaning."[22] Bruzzi then identifies the work of theorist Richard Dyer (particularly how his notion that filmic representations of male heterosexuality are far from stable) as a productive step away from a strict adherence to Mulvey's approach. Bruzzi's point here is of great use in understanding the other guy. Her central claim is twofold, by way of calling into question the absolute adherence to a Mulvian notion of men in cinema, that, "...the spectator is often 'enveloped' by a film's aesthetics but this does not preclude them from also finding themselves distanced from a film, made aware of its constructedness," and that a 'men's cinema' exists beyond traditional masculine cinema types, such as action or spectacle films.[23] Arguably, the other guy as representation of masculinity in film, but also as masculine aesthetic *within* a cinema for men, is a central figure in this new, *non*-action-based men's cinema. Additionally, a great deal of the aesthetics and style of, say, *The Puffy Chair, Knocked Up*, and even a bromantic comedy like *That Awkward Moment* (where the plot circulates around male insecurities and confusion) are borrowed from a genre (rom-com) that is overwhelmingly associated with more stereotypical ideals presented in what is presumably 'women's cinema.' Bruzzi focuses on particular aspects of *mise en scène*, such as costuming, cinematography or editorial stylistic features (slow motion tracking shots of gunfighters, or the pace of editing in an action sequence) in order to point out stylistic consistencies and patterns in men's cinema. Throughout the book, her careful analysis of shot, pace, rhythm, framing, composition and other aesthetic and stylistic choices in men's cinema proves particularly tantalizing to myself and this study, as the bulk of the films I analyze in Chapter 3 are definitively *not* action films. So, while I whole-heartedly agree with her argument and approach (particularly in her emphasis on a more formalist analytics in order to unpack the politics of Hollywood aesthetics themselves), a great deal of my analysis will focus on character and narrative, as the films themselves are more aligned with formulaic, conventional cinematic styles and genres produced for a female audience, and thus often lend themselves to a close reading of these facets. And this in itself is an important aspect of other-guy masculinity, that this transitional identity is being presented to the spectator as something divorced from more stereotypical heteronormative features of men's cinema, including narrative, character as well as *mise en scène*. For instance, an important emblem of men's cinema for Bruzzi is the use of Steadicam (the harness, weight system, viewfinder and camera mount used by camera operators to counteract the shakiness of hand-held shots while retaining freedom of movement), principally when used to capture men walking in slow motion (in a horizontal line, with their back to a fiery explosion, for instance).[24] Notably, the use of Steadicam is kept to a minimum in the mumblecore films I discuss in the next chapter, arguably as a style characteristic of American indie cinema (and thus a rejection of Hollywood cinema, as well as an assertion of an alternate, less gendered filmmaking style) as well as a denunciation (most likely both consciously and unconsciously) of the more macho, mainstream aesthetics of big-budget men's cinema. Of course, the films of Judd Apatow couldn't be more polished and unassuming in their *mise en scène* (and therefore adhere to the more normative strictures of commercially driven, 'invisible' film language). Thus, the other guy and his synaesthetic masculinity remain caught between conflicting impulses to try something different and/or to 'play it straight.' At this point, I would like to turn to an analysis of masculinity studies and its rise to maturity, particularly in regards to the body of the other guy as a site of contestation and uncertainty.

Hegemony, Diversity, Locality

At the outset of the second decade of the 21st century, not only was masculinity in a strange holding pattern, but masculinities as a discipline was also facing some major hurdles, particularly how to conceive of itself as a discipline with its own sub-disciplines. Following the stolen presidential election of 2000, the attacks on September 11 and the second invasion of Iraq, the new left seemed to be thoroughly demoralized, and hence a great deal of forward progress on gender and sexual equality (for women, but also for men) seemed to languish. It was as if President Bush and the new, evangelized right had won the culture wars begun in the 1980s not only at the cultural level, but also at the political and economic levels. This led to the inevitable re-return of the older, white, authoritative male as a kind of benevolent and sagely caretaker, Bush's 'aw, shucks' cowboy mixed with Dick Cheney's technoscientific rationalism, and Rudy Giuliani's acidic sincerity and nationalistic bedwetting. This victory lap was made complete with President Bush's May 1, 2003, landing (in a fixed-wing aircraft, instead of a helicopter, for a more dramatic effect) on the USS Abraham Lincoln, accompanied by an enormous "Mission Accomplished" banner.[25] Bush's nostalgic, Reagan-esque masculinity was on full display, his tight-fit flight suit and pilot's helmet setting up the special delivery—his 'package' figuring prominently by way of several straps criss-crossing his crotch. This dick on display was a kind of premature policy ejaculation, with a substantial number of press reactions highly suspicious of just what was accomplished and when.[26] Against this backdrop, the contemporary left and those engaged in the gender wars in the academy sought to keep the flame of theory alive, so to speak.

To my mind, masculinity studies functions as a series of debates, the first of which focused on nature vs. nurture, primarily as an extension of feminist theoreticians' and practitioners' work in the 1960s and '70s, work that sought to understand men as synchronized products of their bodies and biochemistry, as well as the surrounding patriarchy and its relationship to political economy and socioeconomics. While this debate still persists, it is safe to say that the bulk of theories of masculinity tend to favor acculturation as the more favorable explanation of this dyad. This has as much to do with the rise of post-modernism (polyvocality, significatory elision, the death of the author(ity), destabilization of meta-narratives, etc.), as it does modern men's movements, as well as the close, methodical study of men themselves by sociologically based pioneers such as R.W. Connell (now Raewyn Connell),[27] Marxist polit-ical economists like Toby Miller, and gender performativity theorists such as Judith Butler and David Savran. In U.S. studies of masculinity in particular, it is an oft-used trope to place current masculinities in relation to the cur-rent presidency and their policies, both as a means of teasing out the more insidious factors at work in entrenched masculinities, as well as to highlight the more resistant and subversive forms of masculinity at work in both pop-ular culture and various subcultures. I find this to be a useful tactic, which I will employ occasionally (as I have done above), however it's perhaps obvi-ous to note that each president's masculinity changes considerably over the course of his term, and often is itself a self-reflexive performance of convo-luted disavowal, for example, when President Clinton signed the Defense of Marriage Act in 1996, shortly before becoming embroiled in a sex scandal. I point to the larger (literal) figures of power in the U.S. as a kind of dis-cursive litmus test for a specific reason—there is a tendency with the turn toward 'nurture' (which was really 'turned to' implicitly at the outset of the discipline, and rightly so) to identify group qualities in place of the messy inconsistencies that lie at the heart of most men's daily lives. I am reminded here of the many young white men I see regularly in Los Angeles (and across the country—around the world, really) that have commandeered the mores of black hip-hop culture, whether as a means of disorienting other white men or as a means of playful and performative deconstitution of whiteness itself (or for other, personal reasons). Regardless, I want to emphasize that while both the nature and nurture sides of the debate are essential to any discussion of mediatized masculinity, I tend to favor the understanding of masculinity as a performative, iterative and mimetic strategy, whether it is recognized as such or not by the performer. While many men regard this explanation as a form of dishonesty (presumably a holdover of a more Modernist-centered subjectivity, as well as a form of denial of inconsistency), evidence of this as an accepted tactic and lived daily reality abound in contemporary media. As a strategy and figuration, synaesthetic and performative masculinity are comfortably aligned with theories of acculturation, if not outgrowths that seek to account for inconsistencies in men's behaviors and sense of their own bodies.

R.W. Connell, once Robert, now Raewyn after transitioning from male to female, is commonly understood to be the father/mother of masculinities as an academic discipline, particularly her notion of 'hegemonic masculinity.' If one wishes to trace the birth, adolescence and maturity of masculinity studies (if we have reached a maturity), it is absolutely essential to identify acceptance of and challenges to Connell's notion of 'hegemonic masculinity,' as they serve to illuminate how the field has convulsed and sheared in the face of more distinct and often localized notions of masculinity, as well as how 'hegemonic masculinity' differs from concepts such as hegemonic men, gender hierarchies and masculine embodiment. Initially, the term 'hegemonic masculinity' was appropriated (or extended) from Gramsci's notion of cultural hegemony, or the means by which the ruling class of a society manufactures and maintains its worldviews (so that the status quo functions also as normative discourse), as well as the structure of and dissemination and policing of said ideological framework. Originally, stemming from a Marxist conception of economic class, cultural hegemony attended to social class in a more meaningful and localized sense, so that the hegemony itself was not one of total power concentration at the top (disseminated from there), but consisted of a series of levels and strata that served to inculcate each subject into his position, as well as admonishing him to police others below him in the social and economic hierarchy (enacted here). In this sense, cultural hegemony served to open up social class as functioning in concert with, as Althusser found, ideological state apparatus and its attendant rigidities and dynamics. Connell took this kind of social organization and power intensity to be applicable to masculinity as a type of ruling social caste, particularly in the form of a deeply entrenched mode of idealized masculinity, a masculinity that while not available to every man of every class and social group, still served as a compensatory source of disseminated power for all men. To illustrate this in terms of this project, while the other guy is certainly not the alpha male, he does benefit from the adopted and adapted power he accrues simply by being an extension of a type of hegemonic power, to the extent also that his social construction would have at least nominally involved the inculcation of the privileges of masculinity. (Here would be a good moment to mark your other-guy graphic, perhaps his abdomen or thighs, as they surround and support the phallus—outward appendages of the ideological and physical center.) Hegemonic is a particularly useful term to inspect notions of age and ethnicity, as well as gay masculinity, the most obviously subjugated form of masculinity within the heteronormative matrix of dominant masculinities. If you can't beat 'em, join 'em, as the saying goes.

As Connell's notion of hegemonic masculinity became a widespread term in gender and sexuality studies, as well as a founding principle of academic masculinities, it underwent several challenges and corrections, each of which represent larger shifts in political and social consciousness, as well as more directly linked evolutions within the study of gender, sexuality and men, which in turn represent methodological altercations between sub-disciplines and identity theorists, particularly scholars aligned with the feminist project. A first important challenge to the ubiquity and homogeneity of the concept 'hegemonic masculinity' was 'realness,' or how real men measure up in relationship to the idealization of the male-as-Man within hegemonic masculinity. These adjustments, particularly Collier's important book, *Masculinities, Crime, and Criminology: Men, Heterosexuality and the Criminal(ised) Other*, sought to identify beneficial aspects of masculinity, as opposed to envisioning masculinity as a series of failures and negative traits, particularly in relation to conceptions of the male as predator, violent antagonist and uncivilized threat to the social order.[28] Again, for this study, this approach is useful, as the other guy is a severely conflicted collection of both positive and negative traits (as most men are), with self-awareness and self-regulation as key traits in the daily maintenance of the self and the identity. 'Realness' also shares similarities with the move toward issues of 'embodiment,' or the way men's bodies serve as discursive forces and makers of meaning. By emphasizing embodiment, a deeper inspection of the way men hierarchize themselves and form alliances and allegiances according to body shape, type and ability is possible. Embodiment is a key issue, clearly, for this work, as I'm deeply interested in the *average* body and the way it is represented and accounted for in media, with particular emphasis placed on the body as a site of failure or disappointment, coupled with narcissism and privilege. In Connell's book, *Gender* (2002), the author addresses concerns his previous works had failed to account for, particularly how othered bodies (including transgendered bodies) are theorized and lived in as a literalized form of alterity, while still potentially enjoying the privileges of masculine power. When a body undergoes transformative change, whether through surgery, hormones or age, how is this slippage accounted for, and by, the dominant? These issues are, of course, of particular interest in understanding questions of identity and belonging in transgender persons, whether they are transitioning to or from masculinity. Additionally, morphology becomes an essential ingredient in understanding men if social embodiment is carefully considered—is a skinny, short, (ostensibly) straight, white male afforded the same attention or respect as a tall, muscular, gay, black body? Or vice-versa? These questions can be more fully explored if the social contexts of the other surrounding bodies are taken into account, thus a two-body problem becomes a dynamic system with sensitive dependence on all conditions.

One of the most oft-cited and valuable works dealing with the changing understandings of masculine hegemony came in the form of R. W. Connell and James W. Messerschmidt "Hegemonic Masculinity: Rethinking the Concept," published in *Gender and Society* in 2005. While both authors acknowledge the usefulness and validity of most of the amendments and modifications to Connell's original conception, what is most significant about this article to my mind are the reformulations the authors set out for the future:

> A more complex model of gender hierarchy, emphasizing the agency of women; explicit recognition of the geography of masculinities, emphasizing the interplay among local, regional, and global levels; a more specific treatment of embodiment in contexts of privilege and power; and a stronger emphasis on the dynamics of hegemonic masculinity, recognizing internal contradictions and the possibilities of movement toward gender democracy.[29]

Each of these is a clear recognition of the salience and diversity of these critiques, from locale and localization ("geography") to discontinuity in the subject ("internal contradictions") and so, to my mind, this article serves as a useful summary of the reformulation of the study of masculinities itself, signaling a disciplinary maturity, as well as a re-emphasis of the original motivations that Connell and others set forth decades before: progressive politics, social justice and gender equality. Amongst this blueprint, a central key is struck, one emphasizing that prevailing gender hierarchies, while recalcitrant, must be understood as mutually constative. At heart, this means that women must be theorized, acknowledged and empowered to be part of the formulation, articulation and re-engineering of men's lives, bodies and hearts, as well as within the study of masculinities itself. Thus, feminism and women have been fruitfully re-oriented as ally and conspirator in masculinity and masculinities, with emphasis on the positive relations between communities however disparate. Within the monolith of hegemonic masculinity, alterity and difference are more often shared by men and women than not. It is here that the other guy can be useful as an actual and fictive representation of the relations between men and women (and between men and men), as I argue that *other-guy contingency* (both as group, but also as anti-alpha, eliding manhood) is not incidental, but tactical, and can hopefully be seen as a move toward a productive ground of understanding between the sexes, as well as within the spaces in between the often too-rigid poles of feminine/masculine.

Surrounded, Exhausted and Unloved

A significant and oft-articulated theory of white masculinity involves the concept of crisis, particularly a crisis that the male undergoes as a means of reacting to and navigating what are perceived (by him, as well as by some women) as external threats, stemming from anything from feminism to gays and lesbians, black men to hipsters. David Savran identified a strain of this as "self-reflexive sado-masochism," where the white male sympathetically undergoes physical and emotional torment, hardship and trial in order to complete a kind of self-imposed hero cycle, while also articulating lack as a means of robbing true victims of their victimhood.[30] In essence, the reflexive sado-masochistic process (which Savran identifies throughout popular culture—from Rambo in *First Blood* to the work of Robert Bly) works as a stand-in for a larger socio-political schema as well as a deeply internal psychological 'woundedness'; always a process, never a state. Tania Modleski has also written compellingly about masculine crisis in *Feminism Without Women*, finding that by claiming a kind of cyclical victimhood, men have *narrativized* the 'progression,' utilizing the process of crisis *and* resolution as a means of co-opting the subjugated position.[31] This situation is fraught, Modleski writes, as it means that men have carefully crafted—often with the help of both feminists and theorists of masculinity—the means to create an inherently stable hegemonic process and positionality. Additionally, Susan Faludi's *Stiffed: The Betrayal of the American Man*, takes a similar, if more historicized, view of masculinity in crisis, particularly in that while men may hold the majority of positions of power, individual men shouldn't necessarily be held accountable for the larger class and gender disparities.[32] Faludi, in a very real sense, is offering a kind of apologetics for 'good men,' yet this is easily read as *all men*—taken separately. And so men could be good if separated from other men, intimating that male collectivity is the inherent malaise at the heart of the gender wars. Faludi also finds that men are suffering (she was writing in the late 1990s, during a significant wave of corporate 'downsizing,' 'outsourcing' and middle-class economic stagnation) just as women are—they have lost their jobs, their children and spouses through divorce, as well as their self-respect because of a rapidly changing world that appears to have left them behind. I find this line of reasoning problematic as it further narrativizes crisis and victimization by individualizing and personalizing (mistaking, I think the political *as* the personal) as well as bemoaning either a kind of sacred and tragically absent nostalgic post-war masculinity, and/or an evolving white masculinity that has been dealt an unfair death blow by the culture at large and the economy (particularly the anonymous forces of globalization). If we were to compare this with the rise of the dot-com geek empire builder, as well as the subsequent dotcom bubble burst in the early 2000s, we see a whole sub-species of white middle-class male who were/are beta/omega males by way of their labor sector, as well as potentially ruthless, alpha workhorses (Steve Jobs, the old guard; Mark Zuckerberg, the new). Additionally, Faludi couldn't have seen 9/11 coming and the return of the white male hero and its subsequent nationalist rhetoric as performed by President Bush, Dick Cheney and the other GOP hawks, cowboys and extraordinary renditioneers.

Perhaps the most striking of positions in the masculinity-as-crisis discourse is *Spreading Misandry* (2001), the first in a four-volume set dedicated to identifying and deconstructing misandry within and throughout popular culture, which includes several theories of an ideological-feminist, academic conspiracy against men. So, one immediately gets the sense that this work isn't so much about men and masculinity as much as it is about the perceived 'excesses' of feminists (and women in general), postmodernism, poststructuralism, and critical theory in general. This position is a direct tie-in to more popular notions of the 'crisis of masculinity' and masculine victimology that came to the forefront of masculinities in the 1990s, often casting men (particularly white men) as an endangered species threatened by the massive social, economic and political changes since gay and women's rights became an articulated and enunciated movement popularly thought to be *at odds* with men and their essential truths. In many ways, this situation most likely stemmed from masculinities, as a subject in itself, and the rise of men as subjects worthy of study in the academy. The increased exposure (as this trickled down into the popular consciousness), arguably, has led to an unfortunate situation where men have been re-positioned as victims in relationship to the power they 'once' held. However, I am certainly not saying that men deserve a victim status, but that further understanding of their daily trials and tribulations had the pernicious effect of casting them as subject to their own excesses of power and oppression. In *Masked Men*, Sally Robinson forcefully argues,

> …white masculinity can most fully and convincingly represent itself as victimized by inhabiting a wounded body, and that such a move draws not only on the persuasive force of corporeal pain but also on the identity politics of the dominant. Making a virtue of necessity, the wounded white male stakes a claim to an entire set of cultural conventions originally designed to identify those bodies and subjectivities made to suffer so that white men could retain privileged access to a disembodied norm. Yet such representational strategies can produce unexpected effects—as can analyses of those strategies.[33]

Robinson finds that her feminism is thus accentuated with guilt and culpability (particularly over how the work itself can be misread) as are men themselves, functioning as a buttress for this wounded victimization. However, her prose and arguments are both so clear that, while attending to her objects of study, she often carefully acknowledges the fraught nature of the work itself. Thus, the clarity of her position has, I think, the opposite effect—it clearly, methodically and persuasively exhibits how representations of men are both ingenious and devilish in their constant and dynamic dance with subjugation and dominance, and therefore, her work itself operates as a similar kind of representational tango. If we consider this self-aware and iterative logic as a means to an end, then foundational notions like Connell's 'hegemonic masculinity' are thrown into a new light, consistently negotiating alternating currents of power and powerlessness. And, in terms of this book, the other guy serves an important trope, figuration and physicality that follows this same series of arcs, particularly since the other guy, while often utilizing the victim stance, is also self-aware enough to know that the contingency of his power is based on the contingency of all other men, as well as on the power of women and how they must traverse the popular consciousness. The other guy, in short, isn't the next stage in masculine evolution, but is instead a new masculinity that understands its own contingency and incorporates this into his behavior, with the tacit caveat that masculinity has become a fraught signifier as well as an evolving identity.

Additionally, a slew of new popular-audience books on the 'fall of man' have appeared in the past several years; Suzanne Venker's *The War on Men*, Helen Smith's *Men on Strike: Why Men Are Boycotting Marriage, Fatherhood, and the American Dream—and Why It Matters*, *The Manosphere: A New Hope for Masculinity*, ed. Ian Ironwood, and Jack Donovan's "paleomasculinist" screed *The Way of Men*. In each of these texts, masculinity and men are currently under attack by women, gays, globalism, 'soft' men (surely, this means academics!), the economy, the Obama presidency, even the 'liberal' media itself. This victim-aggressor trope often takes the form of a narrative, where the men are admonished to face these new challenges (because they are *men*!) with the same kind of gusto so often associated with alpha-males and the Greatest Generation. And yet we (a very expansive 'we') have rendered our boys and men unequipped to deal with it, castrating and effeminizing them in our over-litigious, cautionary, wimpy and hyper-regulated culture. As one of the coaches from the Esquire Channel's docu/reality-TV show *Friday Night Tykes* (a show about the hypercompetitive world of a youth football league in Texas for 8–9-year-olds that, in actuality, focuses on the fanatical coaches) states, "We don't hand out trophies for second place. This ain't soccer." Assuming that *all* men want to do what *real* men want to do, these narratives weave a dramatic arc that showcases them taking back what's rightfully theirs and laying down the tried-and-true rules of their fathers, whether it's their jobs (stolen by affirmative action), their wives (they're asking me to clean the house!), their kids (stop crying and shake it off, Timmy!) or their bodies (real men don't use hair gel!). Whereas the study of masculinity (again, think here of the intelligent and generous debates surrounding Connell's 'hegemonic masculinity') has served as a solid model of reorganization and reorientation for men of all types, popular notions of masculinity and men are continuously caught in an oscillating cycle of sensitivity vs. macho-ness, equanimity vs. violence, Paul Rudd vs. Sylvester Stallone.

This push-pull, of course, is the logic of the market, in the larger sense of competition and capitalism, as training ground for robust and strapping nationalist citizen-patriots, and in the more local sense of the disconnected, non-unionized male being shuttled into the potentially objectifying and alienating repetition of the minimum wage slog, with no recourse against exploitation or 'conditional employment' schemes. This push-pull comes from other men, those weaned on the notion of 'personal responsibility' that actually enunciates itself as vociferously anti-'entitlement,' and those raised to understand that women are fundamentally inferior and that other men are best understood as threats, competitors or gay sexual predators instead of brothers, friends, sons and fathers. This push-pull comes from women as well, women who not only accept sexism and misogyny from men as customary, but have come to expect it as 'natural,' and thus become agents of their own oppression. Finally, this push-pull comes from media in the form of advertising, cinema, TV, videogames, webpages and apps, shellacking prepackaged masculine identity and subjectivity onto the proto-consumer, the ready-made desiring machine, so that masculinity becomes the steel beam running from the foundation to the ceiling in the master's house on the hill, inseparable from the formation and composition of the phantasmagoria. However, by highlighting the 'push,' the active and positive strains of masculinity that emphasize and enunciate our connections with other men and women, and all in between, while red-flagging the 'pull,' the lure of sameness, sexism and heteronormativity, we will better be able to identify what segments of the population (and therefore individual men, but also localized communities) offer distinct lessons in radical masculine transformation. If men and the patriarchy are still so vested in their power that they seek to hide the source of it and its performance, then the other guy, by showing his anxieties over it, his willingness to talk about it, can be seen as a kind of evolution, moving toward a space where communication and shared responsibility is an acknowledged aid in the re-distribution of power, even if it is both men and women who must encourage and facilitate this in a 'post-feminist' (read: anti-feminist) culture, a place where seeing and hearing from men doesn't necessarily mean the voices of women are then silenced. In the next chapter, my analysis of the other guy in films, through character, narrative and *mise en scène* will further clarify what he is rejecting, what he stands for, and how his relationships to women can often define his chances for progress, or, at least, whether he sees himself as *capable* of progress.

Notes

1. The film tagline on the promotional poster for the film reads, "He needed a best man…He got the worst."
2. Edward Douglas, "John Hamburg Says I Love You, Man," *Comingsoon.net*, March 12, 2009.
3. Michael Kimmel, *Guyland: The Perilous World Where Boys Become Men*, New York: Harper, 2008.
4. Rich Morin, "The disappearing male worker," pewresearch.org, Sept. 3, 2013. Retrieved Feb. 11, 2014.
5. Mark Hugo Lopez and Ana Gonzalez-Barrera, "Women's college enrollment gains leave men behind," pewresearch.org, March 6, 2014. Retrieved April 2, 2014.
6. Ibid.
7. Eileen Patten and Kim Parker, "A Gender Reversal on Career Aspirations," pewresearch.org, April 19, 2012. Retrieved March 7, 2014. Of course, this isn't a measure of career satisfaction, particularly since the authors also state that the median weekly earnings of salaried or full-time female employees in 2010 was $669 as compared to men, at $824 per week.
8. No author given, "Gender Equality Universally Embraced, But Inequalities Acknowledged," pewresearch.org, July 1, 2010. Retrieved March 8, 2014.
9. Pierre Bordieu, *The Bachellor's Ball*, (Oxford: Polity Press, 2008).
10. Steve Neale, "Screen," in *Screening the Male*.
11. John Ellis, *Visible Fictions*, (London, Routledge, 1982).
12. Neale, 14.
13. Neale, 16.
14. See Schwarzenegger's Muscles, Cyborg Handbook for a deliciously brilliant and twisted reading of the pleasures of Arnold's body.
15. Mulvey, 14.
16. Neale, 18.
17. Neale, 18.
18. Fuchs, in *Screening the Male*, pp. 194–210.
19. Fuchs, 195.
20. Fuchs, 203.
21. Barry Keith Grant, *Shadows of Doubt*, 5–6.
22. Stella Bruzzi, *Men's Cinema: Masculinity and Mise en Scène in Hollywood*, (Edinburgh U. Press, 2013), p. 9.
23. Bruzzi, 15.
24. Bruzzi, 166–167.
25. "'Mission Accomplished' Whodunit." *CBS News*. October 29, 2003. Retrieved November 22, 2012.
26. "Mission Not Accomplished." *Time*. June 10, 2003. Retrieved November 21, 2012.
27. For this manuscript, I have chosen to use 'R.W. Connell' for the material written before Connell completed her sex transition, up to the second edition of *Masculinities* (2005), and 'Raewyn Connell' for materials written after.

28. Collier, *Masculinities, Crime, and Criminology: Men, Heterosexuality and the Criminal(ised) Other*, (London: Sage, 1998).

29. R.W. Connell and James W. Messerschmidt, "Masculine Hegemony: Rethinking the Concept," *Gender and Society*, Dec. 2005 vol. 19 no. 6, 829–859.

30. David Savran, *Taking It Like a Man: White Masculinity, Masochism and Contemporary American Culture* (Princeton, NJ: Princeton U. Press, 1998).

31. Tania Modleski, *Feminism without Women: Culture and Criticism in a "Post-feminist" Age* (New York: Routledge, 1991).

32. Susan Faludi, *Stiffed: The Betrayal of the American Male* (New York: Morrow, 1999).

33. Sally Robinson, *Marked Men: White Masculinity in Crisis* (New York: Columbia U. Press, 2000), p. 20.

· 2 ·

MUMBLING TOWARD ECSTASY

The Other Guy on the Big Screen

"White men are on their way out! Lesbians rule!"
Jay Leno commenting on comic Cameron Esposito's stand-up
set on *Late Night with Craig Ferguson*, September 4, 2013

In a 2013 interview with *The Guardian*, über-stoner and super-slacker Seth Rogen (promoting *This Is the End*, the latest apocalyptic bro-comedy—in many ways an ode to Simon Pegg and Nick Frost's *Three Flavors Cornetto Trilogy*) spoke in his usual offhanded manner about producer concerns regarding the actors essentially 'playing themselves'; "They were like, 'It'll make it less realistic,' and we were like, 'It's more realistic. We're us. There's no break in reality between the world that you as the viewer are in and the world that we are in.'" His emphasis on 'real' is telling, particularly in regards to the other guy. Other guys are always trying to be real. Real with their feelings, real with their actions, even real—in Rogen's case—as an *actor*. Considering that the film also stars Jay Baruchel, James Franco, Danny McBride and Jonah Hill (as well as a host of cameos from the Apatow-Rogen-Paul Rudd-Jason Segal comi-verse), this situation serves as a major signal about early 21st-century Hollywood and masculinity, particularly for these male actors who don't star in action films or feature as traditional romantic leads. These guys are real.

They're on Twitter and Facebook. They do the late night circuit, particularly *The Daily Show* and *The Colbert Report*, and not just during press junkets for their latest movies. They show up just to hang out. In this sense, they're selling an elaborate and carefully constructed image, complete with an average build, close comfort with pot and booze, and very little in the way (relatively at least) of tabloid screw-ups. I draw attention to Rogen's statements to indicate that the other guy, at root, is a dude in search of something, an authentic self. So many of the other guy representations we see on the screen and in other formats depict not only someone who's real, but is keenly aware of their relationship to power edifices large and complex, including how they remain interwoven with ideologies of traditional masculinity itself. In a sense, this emphasis on the real is a careful manipulation of both the viewer as sympathizer and of themselves as subject to larger, always out-of-reach forces, so that in the end, the other guy (like so much of white masculinity) retains a kind of heroic status. Albeit in this case, the other guy is essentially rescuing himself from himself-as-'bad'-masculinity so that he can retain his value to those around him. It's a tenuous and carefully massaged split, a division not wholly unlike a cleft within a victim of Stockholm syndrome—where the captive falls for the captor by way of a tug-of-war of displaced desire and a systematically reconfigured and lauded Big Other.

Rogen continues in the interview to describe his world and how his colleagues are a motley bunch of messy and neurotic guys, sad clowns laughing through the pain, but also straight-shooters when it comes to the *real* them. As Rogen continues to explain his life in Hollywood, one begins to suspect that he and these guys, these *normal* movie stars, have an innate tendency to 'overshare' details of their personal lives (as much of any demographic since the multiplicity of social media growth) as a means of *seeming* to self-evaluate and simultaneously celebrate and abuse their selves, both real and performed (and performed, again, on screen). What is particular here is that, in Hollywood, men have traditionally been expected to give the standard interview, occasionally end up in the wrong bed (or the wrong one, at the right time!), lash out at a director, drink too much at an awards show, etc., but they were never supposed to 'overshare'—truly open up, or they would run the risk of ending up in Woody Allen land. So, what to make of this oversharing, and how does it serve to substantiate and perpetuate narcissistic, synaesthetic masculinity? Is it part of a larger other-guy strategy? American independent filmmaking, long a liminal space for identity transformation and the exploration of gender roles, gives us our first other guy specific genre, mumblecore.

Mumblecore—The Malaise of the Other Guy

The 2002 American independent film, *Funny Ha-Ha*, directed by Andrew Bujalski, is commonly identified as the first film in the 'mumblecore' genre, low-budget, naturalistic films that share aesthetic and formal characteristics as well as thematic similarities. While many of the films are directed by both men and women, the bulk of the films center around young men in various states of what I like to call 'static transition'—where the character is essentially reacting to a situation that has arisen out of his (or, again, sometimes her) inaction. The genre itself was given attention, and summarily named 'mumblecore,' at the regional film festival South by Southwest in 2005 (held in Austin, Texas, since 1987 as a type of alternative to the larger, and increasingly more corporatized, festivals like Sundance or Toronto). Several films, including *The Puffy Chair*, directed by Mark and Jay Duplass, have come to symbolize the movement, particularly in terms of style, form and content. Stylistically, the films feature loosely scripted stories, improvisational dialogue, wavering and regular close-ups of the face, while the stories often explore contemporary anxieties enunciated by failed relationships, personal and social isolation and growing up as an outcast. The name itself comes from sound designer Eric Masunaga, who was referring to films that he had recently completed that were screening at the festival.[1] The name stems from the mumbling that the actors do in the midst of improvisation and how difficult this is to record, with the 'core' attachment demarcating a larger cultural meme-appendage that refers to anything 'hardcore.' Yet 'core' is not used in the sense of 'hardcore porn' as much in the ironic, blasé attitude that Gen-Xers have perfected in order to clearly illustrate that they clearly *do care* about something but are far too cool to emote any of that care (see Aubrey Plaza's or Michael Cera's careers here, both of which have taken the slacker pose to their logical, illogical ends). Thus 'core' is deeply reflective of mumblecore's *emphasis on* its humble production style, rejection of mainstream modes of production, as well as a profligate attempt to back out of any real commitment to radical (or radical-reductive) film making.

In Maria San Filippo's excellent and incisive essay, "A Cinema of Recession: Micro-budgeting, Micro-drama and the "Mumblecore" Movement," she deftly traces the beginnings and maturity (and potential end) of the movement, "With an eye to offering both an observational document and a discursive analysis of mumblecore's aesthetic congruity, promotion and distribution tactics, and reception histories through careful consideration of its origins, ontology, and evolution."[2] In the essay she, "aim[s] more broadly to illuminate how contemporary specialty cinema is adopting impressive strategies of survival."[3] Filippo draws comparisons between mumblecore and to filmmakers such as Jim Jarmusch, John Cassavetes, Gus Van Zandt, and early Steven Soderburgh as well as to Dogme 45's strict rules regarding props, place, light, etc. Perhaps the most astute point is Filippo's enunciation of Ruby Rich's reformulation of the New Queer Cinema in the early 1990s and its status as a "moment" rather than a "movement," signaling the mumblecore directors' distaste for the moniker 'mumblecore' itself. This distaste, particularly in the form of Bujalski's outright rejection of the term, can be explained perhaps by mumblecore's internal and shared ironic positionality in relation to film itself, as well as the film industry (including the press corps that often defines the scope and meaning of patterns strongly in bed with the studios and their cacophonous advertising machines). That said, Filippo continues under the assumption that, like the New Queer Cinema mo(ve)ment, "mumblecore-mobilized and was motivated less by concerted effort or collective ideology than by increased access both industrial and political,"[4] particularly in terms of their work as constantly at odds with mega-slick Hollywood blockbusters, as well as meet-cute indie darlings like *Little Miss Sunshine*. Here, I would like to argue for another term to describe the mumblecore moment/movement—the mumblecore films are less a moment (as a decade is arguably longer than a 'moment,' particularly considering the relative newness of film itself and how historically proximate we are to mumblecore currently), and less a movement (as most of the directors reject the name) than it is an *attitude*. Now, this may seem a small distinction, but the idea of attitude is so very wrapped up in mumblecore, and the other guy, that I feel this distinction will prove useful in the analysis below, particularly since mumblecore is, at root, about other guys and their 'static transitions' from man-child to boy-adult.

Continuing, Filippo points out the importance of the historical moment in which mumblecore flourished, the recession and its post-Bush presidency malcontents. However, I feel that what is more significant about mumblecore's historical exegesis is precisely *when* it started, during the period immediately following 9/11 and at the outset of the DIY movement, both heavily mediated and buttressed by digital technologies, firmly in reaction to Bush's multiple wars and the country's struggle with a fairly sanguine economic period filled with terrorists, the neo-neocons, a postmodern left demoralized by Clinton's sexual escapades and his failures on DOMA and Don't Ask Don't Tell, and mega-products like the *LOTR* trilogy and *The Pirates of the Caribbean* franchise. The folks behind mumblecore, far from being a radicalized movement, I argue were (and still are to a certain extent) reacting to the excesses of digital media saturation (through hand-held and long-take aesthetics) and to the drone of approaching middle age for the Gen-Xers (to which nearly all of the mumblecore filmmakers belong). Filippo touches on this inherent contradiction:

> It may seem rich to offer plaudits to self-involved, only minimally exploited under-achievers who are more disillusioned than disenfranchised, and whose films would hardly seem to cure the ills of our world. In my (and the mumblecorps') defense, however, I submit that these filmmakers collectively demonstrate a degree of humility that is refreshing in U.S. cinema—in speaking only for oneself, in making do with minimal resources, and in portraying life as awkward, messy, and morally complex, in which, to quote Jean Renoir, "everyone has his reasons."[5]

Two ideas stand out here—the idea that the filmmakers are more 'disillusioned than disenfranchised' and that they 'speak only for themselves.' Both of these ideas bear further scrutiny, particularly in regards to the cinema of the other guy.

What I am arguing here, by looking closely at a few films that feature the mumblecore attitude, is that other guy masculinity is not only reflected in the form and content of the films, but that many of these films are quintessentially about the life and times of the other guy. They are an expression of his malaise, body issues, static transitionality and most importantly, his relationship to women and how this shapes their mottled and anxious sexuality. From the film-within-a-film bromance and not-gay, gay sex project of *Humpday*, to the brotherly competition that overruns a family reunion/birthday party in *The Do-Deca-Pentathalon*, mumblecore films set out to laconically, if not always ironically, explore masculinity and the travails of turning into a white, middle-aged, middle-class male, ostensibly one with a heterosexual family and all the trimmings. Here, the filmmakers' anxieties are on full display, even when they are female, with a version of the white-male crisis played out as something fundamentally at odds with not only BIG filmmaking, but with the act of joining BIG Hollywood (or even the indie establishment) as emblematic of the larger selling-out of the obsessively 'unique' Gen-X self, the male that isn't afraid to not be a man, as long as he does it *individually*. Sharing the aesthetics engineered and maintained on Instagram, YouTube and Tumblr, these DIY films and their makers wholeheartedly embrace the digital distribution models and what appears to be a style that shares more with La Nouvelle Vague and Italian Neorealism than Woody Allen and the 'New York moment' movement, while engaging in a gender and sexual politics that shares more in common with college campus laissez-faire idealism and post-Facebook self-infatuation than a radical ethics of the rejection of bourgeois and heteronormative spectatorship in malls and cineplexes across this country and others. When Andrew Bujalski (*Funny Ha-Ha*) initially rejected the term mumblecore, he said, "It makes perfect sense for bloggers to sift through the films and pluck out commonalities," he said. "But the reductive concept that we're somehow the same—that bugs me." Here Bujalski's comment is telling, as it's the bloggers he seems more worried about than the mainstream critics, that his films are for *those* kinds of people, people that blog, people that share the DIY impulse, signaling how embedded this generation of filmmakers and performers is in digital reproduction, distribution, and manipulation, albeit a digital sphere that's built rhizomatically by a distributed network of insiders and culture hackers.

The Slacker Road Trip

In *The Puffy Chair* (2005), the Duplass brothers (directors and writers) open with a scene in an average hipster kitchen, the scene centered around a young white couple, Josh and Emily (Mark Duplass and Katie Aselton—another regular on the indie scene), engaging in an extended session of baby talking, similar to Bill Murray's greens keeper from *Caddyshack* (1980). This shared, intimate lingo is broken by the ring of Josh's mobile phone, which he immediately answers to Emily's frustration, launching into a conversation that at least intimates that he was in a band that broke up, and that he is now in the business of representing other, similar bands (the move from playing to representing in music, and from acting to producing/directing is playful and telling). Emily is livid and storms out, with Josh torn between the call and her, and we sense that this isn't the first time this has happened. Yet, the dialogue, setting and exposition truly take a back seat to the style and aesthetics. One immediately notices not just the camera movement, but the texture of the movement—a combination of unsteady, handheld work mixed with a haphazard zoom (what I call the 'zoop,' or 'damn, I hit zoom...oops!,' where the zoom is so propulsive, it appears to have been a mistake), and wobbly-centered tight close-ups, heads coming in and out of frame. The effect is mildly unsettling, it resembles the final freeze-frame/zoom from Truffaut

400 Blows, where the shock comes from not only Antoine looking at us, but in the zoom's corruption of the magnitude of the sea-scape (along with the filmic/ideological statements of this choice). The intimacy of their space, with them leaning across a dinky kitchen table, is persistently interrupted by the concatenated movement of the camera, implying the presence of the camera operator, if only because the aesthetic is so much a part of the home-video style these fimmakers grew up with, goofy kids playing in the sprinklers in the 1970s while Dad peers through the lens (and also to the extent that one worries about the actor's ability to block out the camera function noises). This also brings to mind Stella Bruzzi's notion of men's cinema as readily defined by *mise en scène*, more so perhaps than by character and/or narrative, and in this case, this stylization marks this film, as well as many other mumblecore films, as improvisational, scruffy and uncompromising, almost hostile to the rigorously structured Steadicam work and viscerally quick editing of action films. Mark Duplass on working on set:

> ...when we discuss quote-unquote the way that we experience life, it's about our vision of where our life is particularly at. It's creating an environment on set that feels as much like real life as possible for the actors. And by that we mean, we don't give them any blocking or specific marks to hit. We try to keep the lights out of their face, keep the gaggle of crew members away from them, so that they feel like they are in a room...where they can go anywhere they want.... There's a camera or two around, and a guy with a microphone, but otherwise, we want them to feel like they're just anonymous regular people doing things. And we find when we foster that environment we get the most naturalistic and, ideally, realistic performance.[6]

So, here, naturalism is key, and the characters, Josh and Emily, seem to be caught in a moment that somehow reflects the greater truth of their relationship, but also the greater truth of their generation's 'real life' itself, or at least an environment that attempts to undo the fabricated nature of film production. Yet, this scene's particular, naturalistic euphoria is quickly shattered by a phone call, one that Josh takes, infuriating Emily as the camera comes to rest on her face. Then, we see the other great truth about their relationship—he's shifty, uncommitted, easily distracted, very much the other guy. It also of course is crucial that Mark Duplass (who plays Josh) is the Platonic ideal of the other guy: sandy, tousled, perfectly un-styled hair, average height (5'10"ish), average build (160 lbs-ish, yet certainly without being fit), articulate, yet oblique about this power as anything other than which to express his needs and feelings, and most definitely blasé about his talent, without being negative or rude. Duplass from an interview for the men's magazine GQ, I assume on independent filmmaking:

> Most people have one independent film in them, because it's so hard. And then
> they're like, "Thank God I made it through. Now I'm gonna go make studio movies."
> Then they keep waiting for studio movies to be made. The thing is, I am willing to
> hang lights and suffer and keep doing it over and over again because I kind of like it.
> It's the same thing that makes you want to go camping. You get into it.

And, so the characters he plays are nearly always a reflection of himself (at least his public persona) and this plays well as a source of authenticity for the films he doesn't direct, write or produce, as well as an extension of an aesthetic of naturalism and for the mumblecore film attitude in general. This is a key point, as Duplass (and his brother) have developed their anti-institutional style not only as a mode of production but also as a mode of identity, and it is this other guy identity that lies at the center of mumblecore. Again, this is an identity that is simultaneously self-obsessed and insular, while keenly self-aware (bordering on pride) of the transient status of the post-collegiate years and the time he has been allocated to 'find himself.'

Returning to the scene, after a brief fight where Emily storms out of the house complaining about Josh's inability to focus and his unromantic disposition, we are then thrust into a road-trip plot line that gently foreshadows the approaching storm of adult masculinity for Josh (Duplass) and his brother (Rhett), as well as how commitment (of all sorts) for men of this generation tends to be frightening and befuddling. In the next scene, Josh convinces Emily to accompany him on the road trip, a journey to pick up a puffy arm chair Josh has bought on eBay, a chair that resembles one his father once loved, in order to deliver it to his father on his birthday. The scene, is, rather lovingly, a direct homage to Cameron Crowe's teenage-love masterpiece, *Say Anything* (1989), specifically to the scene where insider/outsider actor/kickboxer John Cusack holds up a boom-box playing Peter Gabriel's *In Your Eyes*, one of the most parodied and beloved scenes from the John Hugheseque teen romcoms from the 1980s. In *The Puffy Chair*, however, we find Josh on the street in front of Emily's apartment, holding a boom-box which blares a forlorn song from Deathcab for Cutie, the indie band *ne plus ultra* of the 2000s. The film reference and song choice are significant, they indicate both the age of the protagonists to us and remind us that we are/were the same age, using *Say Anything* as common nostalgia signifier. The song also tells the audience 'this is where *we are*, you and me, we *share* this.' A travel montage follows, using the same Deathcab for Cutie song as it crosses from diegetic soundtrack to non-diegetic score, with freeways, signs and the East Coast of the U.S. artfully and lovingly photographed, mixed with a screenshot from MapQuest (these folks are digital, after all).

When they arrive at their first stop to pick up his brother, Rhett, the audience is suddenly presented with close-ups of a lizard filling the frame, as if from a nature documentary. We quickly understand that Rhett is obsessed with filming lizards, and nature in general, without ever mentioning it outside of its context as just 'something to do' with a camera. Serving as a male representation that makes Josh look downright settled and conservative, Rhett is that strange (relatively) new form of hippie, one that champions organic everything, smokes weed and uses hemp, and seems keenly interested in holding the torch that the original hippies once lit, without ever necessarily mentioning them by name. What this new, new-hippie, off-the-grid man is doing is not only rejecting masculinity in nearly all its forms, but rejecting the act of rejection itself. It's more about *being*, really, at places like the Burning Man festival held annually in the Nevada desert, or other multi-day music and arts festivals across the country. However, they are also oddly *digital*, hence the camera. This is probably due to the through line with certain subcultures within their '60s hippie forebearers (Timothy Leary, *The Whole Earth Catalog*). The three 'kidadults' then sit down on the living room floor for a pizza and soda meal like kids after a Saturday soccer game, and Rhett gushes about how happy he is that they are all there, together, to share the meal. Now, Rhett is not an other guy whatsoever, but in terms of the film, he functions as the man who is truly free, so that, as I have mentioned, Duplass' Josh must face his static transition, and appear, subsequently, at least capable of change. Josh is just figuring things out. Rhett doesn't want to figure things out (so, give him a break).

Along the way to the brothers' parents house, a variety of wacky hijinks ensue: Josh lies in an attempt to get a lower price on the hotel room, but is caught by the hotel manager (1 adult per room!), the actual chair is a shabby mess when they arrive to pick it up, and the three end up at Amber's house (a woman Rhett meets at a movie theatre), where Rhett and Amber profess their love for each other and are summarily 'married' by Josh. The movie here hits a confident rhythm, the characters seem well worn, and the cinematography achingly depicts fleeting moments of grace and magic. Yet despite this, Emily (while fairly round as a character, and played with immediacy by Aselton) functions essentially as a tag-along, a nag, or a burden, and Amber is ethereal and unreal, almost a figment of Rhett's stoned imagination. Add to this that Josh constantly refers to Emily as 'dude' (a particularly prevalent trope amongst other guys, which can be read as a male's imperfect attempt to create an equal space, but instead signals a fear of femininity, an erasure of difference, as well as an implied misogyny), and Emily is surreptitiously relegated to the space of 'buddy' instead of girlfriend or romantic partner. In fact, a good deal of the wedding reception seems—while the characters were only drinking booze—seen through the eyes of someone who is pretty damn stoned. I mention this, as marijuana is most certainly a key aspect of mumblecore/other guy-dom—the numbing effect works as a tonic against the outside world's frenetic needs and expectations, while sharing a pipe or a bong is the kind of low-key communal party he doesn't have to put too much effort into. Also, booze is the other guy's father's poison, and the anger that so often comes out of a drunk man is anathema to the true slacker, the other guy in mumblecore land. However, the issue of how female characters are represented in these films (a problem at the core of so much of cinema itself—the female as plot device) presents a starkly problematic concern at the heart of mumblecore, that men have not only directed most of these films, but are often the central characters, with women functioning occasionally as an implied antagonist. This is no more apparent in the early climax of the film and the subsequent elongated denouement.

Towards the end of the marriage reception (comprising only the 5 characters), Josh offers to play a song in honor of their wedding, a sincere and moving song performed while he plays a tiny Casio keyboard. Emily asks why he has never played that for her, with Josh answering that the song was just never 'done,' cueing Emily's fomenting anger but also symbolizing the inherently internal world in which the other guy ideally would like to live, and the world that mumblecore films attempt to externalize—one free from ramifications and deadlines, even if they are personal, intimate. Ending in an argument back at the hotel, Emily lays down the line; she's 26 and fed up with him, "I deserve better than this, Josh." "Better than what? You want me to be this dude that I am not!" What is notable here is that even though Emily is clearly being fair in her expectations, it is she who is still the one 'harshing on his mellow'—if she would just let him be himself, free from the constraints imposed by women, family and culture at large, he would eventually 'get there.' This is transposed against the next scene, the following morning in a diner where Josh, Emily and Rhett sit and discuss what happens next. Rhett says, "I love that girl [Amber], but it wasn't supposed to be," explaining that while last night (the wedding included) was fine and good, it was time for him (and her) to move on, delivered in a sort of post-coital, hippie nonchalance. Emily is flabbergasted, aiming for both the brothers "What is wrong with you guys?! You can't stay married for 24 hours! You can't even say 'married!'" So, here we have Rhett as not necessarily worse than Josh in terms of commitment, but as part of the same masculine continuum of malfeasance, while Emily (and presumably Amber) remain the harpies, regardless of what their *real* needs and expectations are (which seem entirely reasonable, in terms of adult, mature relationships). This series of crises is topped off by an argument between Josh and Rhett, with Josh taking the role of the father, "You're a child. You have no money, you don't know how to take care of yourself!" which of course results in Rhett taking the puffy chair out of the van and lighting it on fire, because of its "bad mojo." Josh then tackles Rhett, breaking his arm in the process, as Emily watches in disbelief. Here we have a double reversal, where sibling rivalry turns into violence, while the (wishfully) domesticated female looks on. Yet it's the freest of the bunch, Rhett, who at least nominally understands that nostalgia always involves pain and sacrifice, and that a puffy chair has now become a stand-in for Josh's search for meaning in his post-collegiate epiphany-less world. Josh completes the reversal cycle by stating, "I can't lead this vacation anymore," perhaps a crafty subtextual replacement for 'I'm a bit tired of trying to find myself.' Yet, it's also a surrender—better that than really fight for it. In a final last gasp of bravado, he threatens the shady upholsterer who quickly fixes the chair and they are once again on the road. So, what kind of male is Josh? Rhett? Even though these two men are far from monolithic men, unchanging juggernauts of masculine stoicism—their alternative masculinities are still subject to these stereotypes, for there is always a power position, whether it is women, other races, children, etc., that sits in opposition. These other guys can be awfully slippery, eliding our suppositions with ironic distance and self-recursivity. A key feature of the other guy, particularly in mumblecore films, is his ability to make static transition seem simultaneously imposed upon him and his choice from the start. So, this masculinity is not only a pretense, but also a strategy that constantly seeks to hide its own motives behind the shield of non-macho tactics.

The three characters finally make it to the brothers' childhood home in Virginia (where was Emily going? Did she go anywhere?) and are met by two perfectly nice, convivial parents (played by the Duplass brothers' real-life parents—again a curious nod to a type of de-sublimated naturalism, but also likely due to the film's obscenely low budget of $15,000). Josh sits down with his dad who advises him on his current relationship woes, which he serenely summarizes in a paternally clever, yet vague manner, "You're either waiting for something really good or really bad to make the decision for you," thus pointing to Josh's internal vagueness and his overreliance on the external for cues, but also tearing open masculinity in general as operating between the opposing forces of positivity and negativity, benevolence and violence, the communal and the instinctual. The film ends with Emily and Josh breaking up, quickly and unemotionally, in a park, circumnavigated by a single hand-held camera. It is terse, unexpected and rhythmically at odds with so much of the rest of the film's meandering pace and themes. Instead of closure and falling energy, the scene, in a way, wanders into an odd final mood, the emotional equivalent of restless leg syndrome. It is an internal itching coupled with a lack of external cause, a distracted and open-ended pull from either far away or deep inside.

Gary Cross, writing in the excellent text *Men to Boys: The Making of Modern Immaturity*, uses the fairy tale of Pinocchio in order to tease out how modern men are able to pursue boys' activities as men and how this has led to a generation of boy-men, men who refuse to grow up. He finds that this process is several-fold:

> The boy-man stands on the treadmill of endless novelty and passively looks for "hits" of pleasure while the adult man cultivates, savors, and gives back. He is skeptical of tradition and puffery and is reluctant to join groups, but in his quest for excitement and a personal reality he cuts himself off from deeper and sustained intimacy with friends and community. Finally, the boy-man remains free and open to change, but, because he sloughs off the past and makes the instant and intense the measure of aliveness, he abandons the possibility of accumulating and savoring experience. The error of the boy-man is not that he does not "act his age" but that he does not grow-up. The virtue of the adult is not that he has matured (meaning reached a plateau) but that he has become independent in a lifelong quest for growing and relating.[7]

I want to touch on several of Cross' points here, particularly how the boy-man relates to the other guy. Having grown up on the California coast, and surfed and skateboarded my way through a great deal of my childhood (are these *thee* boy-man sports?), along with other pursuits and activities, the boy-man is a person I know well, and to be certain, a part of me and nearly all of the men of my generation. So, here, while Cross bemoans this new masculinity that lacks the inherent communal and mature sense of self of the more traditional male, it seems clear to me that the boy-man isn't going to necessarily 'grow up' over the course of their lifetime, simply because the above changes are systemic, ideological and interpersonal. It is a new code shared by men that I know across racial and class divides, both in Gen-X and Y. This new man (particularly on the West Coast) is a tinkerer, an extreme athlete, a techno-junkie, a beer connoisseur, an organic gardener. He is also still a soft-sexist, an open consumer of internet pornography, and often a distracted lover, partner and father. Yet, this expansion of the male domain of activity, emotionality and communication—albeit, much of it is for 'guys only,' or done with a single-minded selfishness—isn't just a rejection of our fathers' sturdy oak stance, but a product of the shattering of masculinity itself in terms of an implied, but often not acknowledged, understanding of the failure of free-market capitalism and effervescent, identity-promotion consumerism. I focus on the other guy in this book because it is a significant masculine figuration for cultural, economic and mediatic reasons aforementioned, but also, in relation to mumblecore films in particular, because the other guy is a sign of (often discontented) effort at making meaning of a changing world in which men have waning power, but also because other guys understand themselves to be boy-men. They seem to know this—whatever 'this' is at the moment—won't work forever. Something's gotta give, and it's probably the other guy. And he knows it.

The second Duplass brothers' film I would like to look at carefully is the *Do-Deca-Pentathalon* (produced in 2008, released in 2012 due to distribution issues), a mumblecore film that focuses more closely on the ageing other guy and delayed adolescence in relation to work and family. Much like *The Puffy Chair*, the film features a festering sibling rivalry, but this time the brothers are grown up, yet can't seem to move beyond a 1990 contest, the Do-Deca-Pentathalon—"25 events, 2 brothers, 1 victor." These two white, middle-class brothers function as effective opposites on the other guy spectrum. Mark (Steve Zissis) is a family man, a pet food salesman, a seemingly good dad and a caring husband who is a bit overweight and aging (and sensitive about it), and so meditates and is in therapy for stress and high blood pressure. His struggle is to navigate the boy-man pull of the past and balance it with the responsibilities of fatherhood, marriage and middle age. He is polite to a fault to his wife Stephanie (Jennifer LaFleur), another reasonable and allowing woman dealing with the exigencies of other guy-hood, as well as a shaggy-haired, pre-teen son (Hunter) who seems destined to continue on the path of his father. Although, as with all pre-teens and teenagers, Hunter generally loathes his dad because, well, that's what you do (hence the not-so-subtle name 'Hunter,' a play on class and traditional masculinity). We are introduced to Jeremy (Mark Kelly) early in the film, an unmarried, professional poker player whose hangdog look reflects a few too many nights in casinos, chasing the big money. Like the other films from the Duplass' brothers' *oeuvre*, the style is similar. *New York Times* film critic Stephen Holden (a self-professed fan of the mumblecore attitude) writes: "The film's casual style works in its favor. It maintains a breezy pace, and much of the dialogue has the spontaneity of expert improvisation. As in the Duplasses' other movies, the narrative momentum is accelerated by quick zooms, abrupt edits and a restless camera." So, it seems clear that beginning with *The Puffy Chair* and in their other films—even the $7 million-budgeted *Cyrus* (2010) staring A-listers John C. Reilly, Jonah Hill, Marisa Tomei and Catherine Keener—that the Duplass brothers have developed and honed a style that is foundational and supersedes (to a certain extent) the thematics or plot of the films. However it is important to note that although *Cyrus* is still a white, middle-class relationship film, the plot circulates around a post-adolescent son's Oedipal relationship with his mother and his efforts to foil her suitor, played by the delightfully schlepy John C. Reilly, so while there is an other guy in the film (Reilly), Hill's character and relationship to his mother is certainly a psycho-sexual alternative to the Duplass' other works.

We are launched into the competition near the start of the film, where Mark, Stephanie and Hunter are set to participate in a charity 5K fun-run, a family tradition on Mark's birthday weekend. Jeremy, upon hearing about the fun-run, immediately drives his muscle car right up to the race start and sprints off to catch up to Mark, who upon seeing him, picks up the pace, leaving his son and wife behind (as a first indicator of what truly matters to Mark, clearly). After the race, featuring a diving finish onto concrete by both brothers (Jeremy wins by a nose), we find Jeremy alone in his mother's house (Alice, played by Julie Vorus), nostalgia-tripping through the remnants of his youth (trophies, mementos, etc.), searching specifically for a videotape of the original 1990 Do-Deca-Pentathalon, which to his dismay has been taped over with a yoga instructional video (oh, the emasculation!). It's important to note that Mark unofficially 'lost' the original because their (now-dead) father pulled him out of the water during a 'holding-your-breath' competition, hence their father's anxieties about his son's safety has set in motion an almost diabolical rivalry between the brothers. Thus, Mark has been relegated to the status of 'momma's boy' (and the father to the status of unwelcome interloper in each male's destiny and development—a rejection of the father if there ever was one). The middle third of the film is dedicated to the brothers locked in battle in a variety of comic and often ludicrous challenges: pool, ping pong, laser tag, arm wrestling, basketball, racquetball, go-karts, mini-golf, push-ups, air hockey, etc., so many of which are the normative realm of adolescents, but which are pursued by middle-age men and their middle-age bodies, to high comic effect. Yet, more sinister forces begin to bubble to the surface.

While Alice, their mother, seems a bit out of touch, she still understands the contest as inherently bad for her sons, but tends to take the 'boys will be boys' attitude that marks her Baby Boomer attitude toward men in general. However, Stephanie is outspoken, articulate and intelligent and cares for Mark's failing health, and even more so, hates Jeremy and what his presence does to Mark, indicating years of foment and frustration. Hers is the anger typically leveled at the other guy—not so much at his 'typical guy' routine, but instead at his fairly progressive male maturity skewed with his inability to *act* on that maturity. And, the stakes are higher for Mark than any of the other guys we've looked at so far because he has a growing son, a mortgage and a body wracked by stress caused by the internal confusion of the new masculinity. So, in order for the competition to continue unabated, the brothers agree (with a secret meeting and a handwritten contract) to keep the competition (all to occur in a weekend—a birthday weekend, to boot) under the radar (of the women). And, of course, they request the aid of Hunter who has taken a frustrating (for Mark, at least) interest in Jeremy, because Jeremy sits up late with Hunter crank-calling, and because he really "talks to him." This is galling to Mark, and Jeremy disparages Mark's failing fatherhood and body in a scene where he finds Mark taking pills late at night. Jeremy asks, in typical guy-speak, "Dick broken? Hair pill? Log jam? Shitting rivers? You depressed?" managing to push nearly all of the middle-aged male health crises and the relevant pharmaceuticals (erectile dysfunction—Viagra; hair loss—Propecia; etc.), finishing with the most emasculating of them all, depression. For depression means that the male is questioning *himself*, as well as seeking treatment (instead of 'manning up') and taking a pill that robs him, in the world of men, of his sacred free will and individuality.

Throughout the contest, we continue to see Mark's body failing, but also Jeremy's. However, it is Mark who shows it, while Jeremy 'takes it like a man.' These trials bring to mind the work of Deborah S. David and Robert Brannon, particularly *The Forty-Nine Percent Majority: The Male Sex Role*, where the authors spell out four central rules of masculinity, all pointing back to the male body as the site of its performance of power. They are as follows: No sissy stuff, a real man is a 'big wheel,' a real man is a 'sturdy oak,' and a real man will always 'give 'em hell.'[8] What's striking about this list, given that it was written in the mid-1970s, is that these rules are still widely acknowledged, with certain telling caveats. While the language is a bit dated, men are still admonished to achieve, pursue and fight for their place in the world, in a constant cycle of proving. What stands out contemporarily, particularly for the other guy, is that 'sissy stuff' has now largely been redefined. With the rise of geek culture as cool culture, the growing foodie movement, and the phenomenon of 'manscaping' (or, male grooming), what was previously seen as 'sissy' has gained acceptance, particularly considering the success of shows like *Queer Eye for the Straight Guy* and a number of cooking shows and competitions (*Master Chef*, *Top Chef*, *The Naked Chef* and the like). Regardless, both Mark and Jeremy, through the competition, as well as through their lives, have chosen to follow some of these (quite dated) rules: Mark may sell pet food, but still, he's a salesman, the territory of the self-starter and go-getter, and Jeremy is a poker player, a grown-up game that rewards risk, calculation and 'balls' in order to climb to the top.

Inevitably, their competition can't sustain itself, end well or remain hidden. Mark skips his own birthday party in order to complete the Do-Deca-Pentathalon, incensing Stephanie. Finally, after Mark suffers a minor mental and physical breakdown where he, emasculated and domesticated, dribbles a basketball and dunks the ball furiously in front of the family looking a bit like Godzilla destroying a city, he walks off in a huff with Jeremy in tow, in an effort to calm his wounded brother. Jeremy finally finds Mark, adolescently slumped on a curb in front of a Quickie-Mart, enormous Slurpee frozen drink in his hand. Mark confesses that he wants Jeremy's life. Jeremy confesses the same. "Can't believe I let this happen. Can't believe I got so fat," blurts Mark in a moment of self-reflection and apologetics. Mark's wounds and self-doubt come directly from his body and his natural—*natural*—progression into a different phase of life, and into a different kind of body with different abilities.

Because this mumblecore film focuses on the latter stages of the other guy's journey toward maturity (or is this as mature as they can get?), it's significant for this project in that it highlights how deeply central the body is to the male and the masculine experience. However, where many other men, particularly men in their 20s, are often portrayed in the media as able to constantly maintain an almost surreal level of fitness (watch any daytime soap opera or nighttime drama and notice the men when shirtless, regardless of age), the other guy is fully aware and at odds with his distinct lack of ability or motivation to pursue fitness for itself, in itself. Instead, the expectation is that the body will always remain 'on tap,' ready to perform at the levels of youth. For both Jeremy and Mark, that was 1990, and their test was and is the Do-Deca-Pentathalon. What is a minor victory for these two men, and for other guys everywhere, is that there wasn't a winner crowned in the film, signifying perhaps that with age may come realizations about the body, shared responsibility, unreasonable male media models and competition itself.

The Apatow Effect

Producer, director, writer and general go-to guy, Judd Apatow has firmly established himself not only as a voice for outcasts, geeks, and most importantly men in Hollywood, but also as a brand in himself. The Internet Movie Database often uses the term 'Apatow-esque' in their description of his films, as well as many other films that fall into several categories: rom-com, 'bromance,' outsider comedy, quirky comedy. etc., and Netflix has an entire category (based upon the user's interests) entitled, "If you like Judd Apatow, you might like…" Apatow's work tends to focus on relationships (almost exclusively straight), white folks in the middle class, and the trials and tribulations of growing up in an increasingly alienating and ideologically manipulative world. So, in this sense, his characters are often self-aware and internally at odds with their external circumstances. In the critically lauded *Freaks and Geeks*, which Apatow executive-produced, the stories hone in on teenage alienation and malaise, often featuring touching, searching stories and dialogue. His production style is clear to be sure, unfettered by artistic excess or style, and yet it performs the versimilitudinous trick of erasing (or at least hiding) the mode of production so that the characters, writing and scenarios become the central focus. *Freaks and Geeks* was also responsible (in just its one season) to launch the careers of long-time Apatow favorites Jason Segal, Seth Rogen, and James Franco (Apatow, after dropping out of USC during his sophomore year, also lived with Adam Sandler), and thus has achieved the status of Apatow-primer and origin story (although before this Apatow had already enjoyed critical praise for *The Larry Sanders Show*). What is key for this study is Apatow's handling of men and, in particular, his responsibility for tracing out and representing so much of what constitutes the other guy. In films like *The 40-Year-Old Virgin*, *Knocked Up*, *Forgetting Sarah Marshall*, and *This Is 40*, Apatow has created a body of work that has not only reflected the changing attitudes of middle-class white males from adolescence through middle-age, but has in many ways prescribed his world, attitude and mores, what I refer to as the 'Apatow effect,' a central aesthetic in synaesthetic other guy masculinity. Tamar Jeffers McDonald, in the essay, "Homme-Com: Engendering Change in the Contemporary Romantic Comedy," explores the new male-centered rom-coms, particularly the way that the films treat sexuality, and by extension, women's sexuality in these films (as well as earlier rom-coms aimed at women). She aptly terms these the "sex-averse Ephroneque competitors."[9] McDonald finds that bodily humor and disgust are at the heart of these brom-com films, as a means of appealing to men's more prurient interests, but also as a means for narrative and sexual closure that, in turn, emphasize a more conservative, monogamous, sexuality-as-love.

> Narrative closure within this new grouping of films is only achieved by a capitulation to monogamy, the same outcome promoted by the dominant form of the genre, the very films the boy rom-com appears to be contesting. Across both the sexier and more romantic strains of the male-centered rom-coms, an amelioration of hedonism seems inevitable: again and again the heroes, the winners, are the men who give up their randy, irresponsible, immature ways, to have meaningful sex with one woman.[10]

Here McDonald is arguing that the presumptive edginess of bromances are essentially subverted by the strict adherence to sexual monogamy, and through extension, the male body within the bromance becomes the site of contestation, the wild space that must be tamed. For the other guy, this extended adolescence and refusal to sexually 'cool it' is made literal by the 'man cave' from which he refuses to emerge, happily playing with his buddies. No girls allowed. However, as we will see in Apatow's films, this narrative closure isn't as pat as McDonald put it; more often than not, the central male retains his freedom through his capitulation, as this can be read as a tactic of acquiescence in order to keep playing the game.

In his incisive essay, "I Love You, Man": Bromances, the Construction of Masculinity, and the Continuing Evolution of the Romantic Comedy," John Alberti analyses the contemporary romantic comedy, particularly bromances (films where the relationship between two heterosexual men—bros—supersedes either of their relationships to women) in relation to the constantly morphing nature of the romantic comedy genre. He writes;

> I argue that these films can also be understood as engaging self-consciously with both the "perfectly codified conventions" of the traditional romantic comedy and with

conflicting representations of masculine identity connected to these conventions. In these movies, we find male characters confused and even frightened by what they experience as destabilized codes of gender identity as well as the pathological nature of many of the more conventional versions of these codes.[11]

Alberti finds that these films both engage with the traditions of the romantic comedy genre while simultaneously acknowledging that the masculinities at work in these films are themselves problematic, particularly when one considers the rigorous codification of heterosexual norms and structures found in so many Hollywood romantic comedies (boy meets girl, boy looses girl, boy gets girl). He goes on to write how the men in these movies (so often the other guy) are consistently befuddled by what they see as shifting gender codes (the increasing power and mobility of women, in particular) as well as how constricting and "pathological" masculine codes are in the world of the film. Yet, the films, Alberti argues, are "engaging self-conscious" on multiple levels, and so the films themselves are a way to work through, particularly for men as audiences, the pathologies to which they are subjected. Bromances, therefore, are representations of this real-world struggle while they concurrently buttress masculine bewilderment. This point is key, for the victim status of the other guy, overwhelmed and underwhelming, becomes a part of the self-conscious nature of masculinity in these films, but is also reinforced through the act of watching these films. Alberti continues;

> These observations are not meant to deny the androcentric and even misogynist cultural logics at play in these movies but to suggest another way of understanding their particular versions of objectification and gender panic in terms of the current moment: as part of a project of reconstructing the heterosexual romantic comedy male hero, a hero who preserves the logic of heterosexual desire but who also questions the very subject position of masculinity itself within the romantic comedy.[12]

And so the momentum of the other guy—his struggle to adapt to a changing world, and yet continually rely on the victim position while he simultaneously disavows it—as precipitous and halting as it may be, is reflected in these films, but also, more importantly, not as a simple reaction to masculine "gender panic," but embraced as a mode of representation (or performance) itself. And while Alberti identifies the male protagonists in these films as the "male hero," I would suggest that these men are in fact a new type of hero. Instead of anti-hero, they function not only as an *alt-hero* (after the alternative music scene, but also as a respectful riff on the sub-altern, to the extent of course that the other guy sees himself as victim), moving the plot forward as the traditional hero would, but never making truly heroic choices, still getting some version of the girl, but not without the aid of his buddy (hence bromance). Here the classic Campbell hero's journey is turned on its head, so that the 'helper' or 'aid' to the hero doesn't keep him on the path of sacrifice and rebirth. Instead, in these films—the buddy, the bro—serves as a bifurcative agent, steering him away from the true test (and directly toward the solution, and the woman), so that the alt-hero surmounts the obstacles *through* his heterosocial (often careening off the dual poles of the hetero-erotic and homophobic) romance with his buddy, the *other*-other guy. The Duplass brothers certainly deal in alt-heros and question the norms of the romantic-comedy genre, and Apatow further complicates the genre to the point of 'hashtagging' it for himself (and his buddies, including many of the women in the films).

In his book, *Shadows of Doubt: Negotiations of Masculinity in American Genre Films*, Barry Keith Grant finds that both masculinity and genre in film function similarly, in that, "…masculinity in American cinema, indeed, like all cultural categories of identity, has never been monolithic or stable; rather it is an always shifting concept."[13] It is precisely this shifting nature in relation to strict codes that dictates how and when genre and masculinity slowly morph according to cultural, institutional and economic norms and challenges. Grant continues;

> Hollywood's traditional reliance on sequels, prequels, remakes, series, and cycles, which has characterized its film production throughout its history and continues unabated today is only the most obvious testament to this ritual function of genre. Genre conventions depend for their existence on their serialized repetition, and in turn this repetition allows individual genre movies to partake of, to modify, to question, and to subvert their generic traditions and the ideology they have tended to endorse. No genre is inherently reactionary or progressive.[14]

Grant makes a strong and articulate case for the inherent connection between masculinity and the genre film without arguing that, "the history of American cinema [is] as a series of masculine crises" (a position he finds both "inappropriate" and a serious "misunderstanding" of Hollywood film). And so I would like to utilize this central argument in order to argue that Apatow films are a genre unto themselves, and the subsequent quality of masculinity that we see in them is a product of this genre-ization. I would also argue that many of his films (along with many mumblecore films) are a form of self-substantiation for the other guy himself, in form, content and ideology, one of the central syn-aesthetic ingredients. In *The 40-Year-Old Virgin* (2005), *Knocked Up* (2007), and *This Is 40* (2012), all three of which Apatow wrote, directed and pro-duced, Apatow has created what I like to refer to as the Sperm Trilogy. In the first film, Steve Carrell plays a man who, it seems, has never seen sperm, Seth Rogen in *Knocked Up* has no concept of what sperm does, and Paul Rudd, in the sequel to *Knocked Up*, *This Is 40*, is faced with just what sperm can do. In each film, the protagonist seems mystified about relationships, women, other men, sex, pregnancy, children and most importantly his status as a male at the start of the 21st century.

In *The 40-Year-Old Virgin*, Steve Carell plays Andy Stitzer, an electronics salesman living a life of involuntary celibacy, seemingly without any wor-ries. He collects action figures, plays videogames, rides his bike to work and is kind to his elderly neighbors. The film begins with an establishing shot of a middle-class apartment building, and quickly cuts to a shot of Andy (Steve Carell) in bed in the fetal position, clutching a pillow between his arms and legs, a stand-in for a partner, presumably a woman, dredging up the couples sport of 'spooning' as well as a mild Oedipal refuge.

His bedroom is littered with carefully placed action figures (from *Star Wars*, *Star Trek*, action films and TV, etc.) as well a massive wall-sized illus-tration of a spaceship resembling the Millennium Falcon from the *Star Wars* franchise. Next we see Andy in profile, sporting a full erection creating a tent out of his boxer short underwear. He seems oblivious except when he urinates, so that he must contort his body ever forward, to comic effect, in order to get the urine in the toilet. The quotidian elements of this and the rest of his morning routine (exercising on various contraptions, a perfectly cooked omelet with bacon and fresh fruit, eaten alone in his kitchen) all hint at a loneliness, but also a calm, gentle masculinity caught in the throws of a post-adolescent quagmire (virginity, et al.), particularly in relation to Carell's peaceful characterization and middle-age look and physique. After riding his bike to work (with pant leg carefully tucked into sock and a safety helmet), we see that his work life at an electronics store (SmartTech) where he works in the stock room, is much the same. Yet instead of (since this was well after the downsizing debacle of the '90s, but before the 2008 recession) Andy filling the narrative position of the middle-aged male who *failed* at something, it seems clear that the truth is he hasn't *succeeded* at anything, or at least hasn't tapped into his masculine potential in order to 'visualize' success (in proper West Coast proactive lingo). Here we meet the cast of characters that populates this film, some of whom also appearin *Knocked Up* and *This Is 40*, Paul Rudd in particular (who becomes the star of *This Is 40* as a more meaningful, less absurd version of Andy's Peter Pan complex). There's David (Paul Rudd, playing the broken-hearted romantic with anger issues), Cal (Seth Rogen, as usual, the stoner with a name that plays on the stereotypical California slacker dude), Paula (Jane Lynch, playing the supervisor and early version of the on-screen 'cougar,' or sexually voracious middle-aged attractive woman), Jay, the African-American 'player' (Romany Malco), and Mooj (an older, South-Asian man, presumably playing the educated foreigner forced to work under his paygrade in the U.S.). A good deal of the film revolves around Jay, Cal, and David goading Andy into action, sexual and otherwise. Andy is the type of male who, because of how kind he is, doesn't fit into the male, smack-talking, misogynist, cocksure group, that is, until they find out that he is a virgin at a poker game—a game Andy would have never been invited to had the men not desperately needed another body in a chair to effectively play cards. Cal describes Andy, "He's a nice guy, but I'm pretty sure he's a serial killer," in reference to how calm and 'normal' looking he seems, pointing to masculine normative conceptions of male behavior—if you don't 'give it' and can't 'take it' (verbally, socially, sexually, with a hint of homoeroticism always just beneath the surface), there's clearly something amiss. Andy is forced into a heterosexual rite of passage during the poker game when they question his sexuality, "I'm not gay. I've been with tons of women," engaging in the 'I'm-not-so-I-am' logics of heterosexual homophobia. He continues, "I respect women. I love them. I respect them so much I stay away from them," confusing fear of the 'mysterious, exotic' feminine Other with a kind of soft-feminism. Such is Andy's world, and the world of many straight men—bewildered by women in general, confused by the new rules, opting out in order to nurture their familiar identity and 'simplified' lifestyle.

A pathetically hilarious montage follows where we see a typical, wild night (alone) at Andy's house: playing videogames, singing karaoke, laughing hysterically while reading comic books, playing the tuba, and painting metal mini-figures created for table-top role playing adventure games, all the realm of the 'normal' male teenager, but increasingly the realm of adult male other guys, often as a means of 'getting away' from their partners and families (which becomes a central trope in *This Is 40*). In a later scene with David (Paul Rudd, showing his uncanny knack for representing the other guy as a series of contradictions), Andy gets advice from David, who spins a story of his lost love (a two-month-long relationship, now two years passed) and how it is important for women to have "space" and to respect their "journey," before he breaks down into a bile-filled, cynical sexist rant (here, Rudd functions as the male 'helper,' both narratively and masculinely, the root of the bromance explored in other Apatow films). Andy seems further confused in the following scene when he is shown walking down the street, near hysterical over the 'onslaught' of objectively framed female body parts which seem to be following and filling his gaze, finally ending in an overwhelmed sense of anxious repulsion. Yet what seems to confuse him after David's new-age tinged advice and rant are not women themselves, but the parts of women he is unfamiliar with or is privy to, to the extent that the female body is degraded to a series of curves and holes rife with psychosexual damnation. This is a typical trope for all three films, to the extent that it seems that Apatow uses this technique to seem edgy in his raunchiness, but which belie a sexist, conservative, traditionalist mindset that reflects gender mores usually associated with the 1950s. This is compounded with a series of Andy's bizarre, failed-sex dreams and attempts at fantasizing in order to masturbate (complete with candles, Lionel Richie's "Hello" and family picture frames laid flat, out of view) where the female is either a succubus, a bitch or a slut who slowly morphs into a female figure speaking with Andy's voice, so that Andy is, in the end, seducing and taunting himself in a weird auto-erotic trance/avoidance dance of misplaced sexual desire, unfettered misogyny and erotic self-loathing/love.

Coming to a head, Andy is taken to the bars by his friends where he is attacked by a very drunk woman, Nicky (played by Leslie Mann, Judd Apatow's real world wife, featured in all three Sperm Trilogy films), who proceeds to drive while intoxicated, yell at him/hit on him, and smash into another car, which then prompts her to throw up all over him, finishing with, "You can still have sex with me." Exemplary of Apatow's work, we see the other guy caught in a scenario where a woman serves as a personification of Andy's fear and confusion, effectively the cause of his celibacy and anxiety, a tautological excuse to live the life of the heroic other guy, ostensibly away from the impurities of the female gender. Cal delivers a similarly toned speech to Andy regarding why he should have sex with multiple partners he doesn't care about before he does with someone he cares about: "You are gonna be so bad at sex the first time, you don't want to have sex with someone you like… you wanna have sex with hoodrats so by the time you get to the girl you do like, you're not going to be terrible at sex." Both of these scenes presuppose something key—that the purpose of sex is to prove your worth as a male and that you will lose the valued mate if you don't perform. Additionally, it posits a whole disposable class of females ('hoodrats,' a term taken from hip-hop music and culture, denoting an unattractive woman—'rat'—from the 'hood') whose function is for sexual 'practice.' This is part of the Big Lie of masculinity, that females 'ranked' beneath you in attractiveness will automatically sleep with you, similar to the sizing-up men do when walking into a room; which men are smaller than me or bigger than me physically, effectively 'whose ass can I kick (and whose can't I)?' Later in the film, Andy gets advice from Cal on another male-female romantic skill—talking to women—where Cal opines, "It's all about talking to women. The problem most men have is that they just plain, straight-up don't know how to talk to women. Women just want to talk about themselves. Ask them questions." Andy, of course, literalizes this advice and upon approaching a woman in a bookstore, proceeds to, in almost perfect Socratic method, respond to each of her questions with another question, turning questions into sexually tinged declaratives obliviously, so that each question he asks becomes a reversed displacement of her assumed desire. This is, after all, how the other guy performs romance and sexuality, as a series of mirrored acts in the hopes of saying what the subject of desire actually wants, a sort of lazy psychoanalytics that evacuates both his agency and his literalized desires in favor of not 'rocking the boat.'

The 40-Year-Old Virgin unfolds narratively in a traditional, very conservative fashion, where Andy meets the 'real' woman, Trish (an always beguiling Catherine Keener), and proceeds to woo her, losing her in the process because of a series of misunderstandings, eventually winning her back in an act of reckless bravado. Often, these scenes are fabricated as stand-alone comic bits, not necessarily moving the narrative forward, in what has become a familiar Apatow mode—a raucous scene where body functions, sex, drinking or male bonding form the backdrop for many of the actors to improvise their dialogue, relying on their (often obviously actorly) comedic chops.[15] In this sense, Apatow isn't so much scripting an inherently funny film as much as he is casting effectively, hence his use of the same actors again and again (think back to the remarks by Rogen regarding 'realness' of the acting at the start of this chapter). In *The 40-Year Old Virgin*, these kinds of scenes are played against other scenes where Andy navigates his sexual awakening, serving as a running commentary that links the viewer to Andy's narrative (and sexual) quest. For instance, Andy tries and fails to put a condom on for the first time, thoroughly and naïvely amused at their shape and utility. After Trish's teenage daughter and boyfriend walk in, thus interrupting their encounter, Andy calls the (presumably) Viagra helpline, asking for advice regarding "an erection that lasts more than 4 hours," we are forced to acknowledge that Andy considers this erection different than the one he has every morning, in that this one was caused by someone, and so is framed as unnatural and beyond his scope of understanding. Andy's other guy is then configured as one who takes care of his body (exercising, eating well), but doesn't understand it in relation to other bodies, particularly women's bodies and the 'effects' their bodies may have on his. However, along with this physical perplexity comes a new found confidence and Andy is promoted to salesman at work, eventually reaching manager (wearing a suit and tie—the entrée into white-collar respectability) and, with Trish's help, begins to pursue his dream of opening his own business. But, in order to do so, he must sell his still-packaged action figures in order to secure seed money for the business, which he does with great reticence, as we watch him literally package and ship off his childhood and stalled maturity. Of course, he lashes out (albeit, kindly) at Trish, to which she responds, "I'm trying to help you grow up!" Facilely positioned as the nag and bitch, Trish begins to question Andy's intentions (as well as his sexuality), "Andy, I'm throwing myself at you and all you can think about are fucking toys!" Andy has redeemed himself prior to this (for failing to 'seal the deal') by endearing himself sincerely to Trish's children, Marla and Julia, particularly in a scene where he volunteers to take Marla (the teenager) to what appears to be Planned Parenthood (although it is never referred to this way, instead called a 'clinic') and during a group information session appears thoroughly confused by all things sexual, including a model of the female reproductive organs. Marla, slyly played by Kat Dennings, is a savvy teenager and asks him in the car on the way home if he is a virgin. After he asks how she knew, she responds by saying that she goes to school with hundreds of 'horny' boys and knows what boys want. This is framed against Trish, a single mother whose oldest daughter now has a child (making her, as the boys say, a 'hot grandma'). These scenes and details reveal a hypocritical undercurrent in Apatow's films, that women seem to be sexually more advanced, knowledgeable and developed, have access to affordable and compassionate health care (including birth control), supply the condoms and insist on their use, and see pregnancy and children as the fulfillment of their sexual (and biological, and cultural) purpose (this last point will become more apparent in the next two films). This can explain the three films' successes—they provide more conservative viewers with just enough family values to not offend while piquing their prurient predilections, and present a happy mirror image for more liberal audiences with their middle-class, California bo-bo ethos, faux inclusivity and multi-culturalism.

This is not to say these are *bad* films. More accurately, they are ideologically unconflicted in their presentation of gender relations to the extent that the Family remains the final endpoint, and beyond that (more subtlety), so too does middle-class consumerist, ironic alienation—the space where the other guy, the alt-hero, is both victim and savior. Trish, cradling the mildly injured Andy after a bike accident, near the end of the film, comments on his fear of sex with her, a woman he cares about, saying, "Of course it'll be good… we love each other." It is dialogue like this that evinces Apatow's central concern—that people (straight, white people, at least) need each other and that life has a natural progression to it, and there's really no fighting it— a kind of apoplectic eschatology born and bred in the suburbs. In the final scene, however, the audience gets an absurdist surprise, fracturing the pat rom-com narrative (that is, of course, after Trish and Andy are married and have sex on their honeymoon, so that Andy, dressed in white, is effectively turned into the virgin bride): the cast prance and sing "Age of Aquarius" from the hippie-musical *Hair*, signifying a second era sexual awakening for Andy. It turns out that an other guy having sex for the first time qualifies as a cultural revolution.

Knocked Up: The Other Guy Gets Pregnant

Knocked Up (2007) features much of the same cast, comedic business and life philosophies Apatow had explored in *The 40-Year-Old Virgin*, and it's here where we begin to see this Hollywood cadre's conception of themselves as purveyors of a brand and ideology. Loosely stated, the film follows the boy-meets-girl, boy-loses-girl, boy-gets girl structure nearly literally, but with an important exception—an initial 'hook-up' between Ben (Seth Rogen) and Alison (Katherine Heigl) ends up with a pregnancy, the catalyst for Apatow's family values message staged in the film. We also begin to see the ossification of the unlikely heroes of the Apatow world, comics/actors Jason Segal, Jonah Hill, Martin Starr and Jay Baruschel settle into roles first solidified in *Freaks and Geeks* and other films/shows. But what is striking here is that each of the actors' characters names is their own. Much like *This Is the End* (2013), it seems that these other guys, these Hollywood 'outsider' other guys (largely because of their body types, Jewishness, and casual likeability), have so thoroughly invested in making their on-screen personas concomitant with their off-screen personas (particularly in press-junket interviews) that a peculiar insistence on a kind of (masculine) authenticity begins to appear mildly pathological. It is as if, by fusing their on-screen/off-screen selves (or by erasing the difference), they become emblematic of not only the 'realness' of Apatow's world and characters (which, of course, are heavily buttressed by scripts that rely on improvisation), but of the other-guy-as-symptom as well. What I mean to say here is that the heavily mediated masculinity both on and off screen of the other guy is a product of those on-screen representations as more *real than the real*, in a near perfect inverse Baudrillaridan elision, so that the on-screen other guy is somehow the more authentic of the two. And so what does this mean for the everyday, real-world, non-Hollywood-famous other guy? By witnessing the Apatow crew's inter-mediated authenticity, the other guy must necessarily accept this aspect of other guy-ness as not so much the referent or a Platonic ideal, but instead as an extension of a naturalized gender performance, one that finds its authenticity in the rejection of overt performances (even if they are on screen!). In an important sense, this serves as an extension of Judith Butler's conception of heterosexual melancholy.

In *Gender Trouble*, as well as in *Bodies That Matter*, Butler forcefully theorized gender as an effect, one constituted of and maintained by iterative acts that create the appearance of a stable or static gender, a *performativity* that is in itself a form of discursivity (as opposed to *performance*, which I take to mean a self-conscious act, mimesis or fantastic creation of an alternate, assumed persona or character). This contract is theoretically (and practically) signed by all those who have a stake in its stability, and is therefore an investment in their place in the binary gender system. Butler writes, "…the tacit agreement to perform, produce, and sustain discrete and polar genders as cultural fictions is obscured by the credibility of those productions—and the punishments that attend not agreeing to believe in them."[16] At the core of this gender performativity, more particularly here in male-identity performativity, is the inability to grieve the loss of (or ability to identify with, but also to attach to) the parent of the same sex, and so the male must engage in gender performances that allegorize (and perhaps also disavow) the contravened love. Heterosexual melancholia is the result of this inability to grieve. I bring up Butler's compelling schema for several reasons. The first is to highlight that the lost love for which we are unable to grieve contains within it the shadow of the erotic, hence so much of compulsory male heterosexuality is comprised of homosexual disavowal, to a certain extent because of the inability to grieve, but also because melancholia itself is a passive response, unacceptable to the mantras of masculine action and proving. Second, heterosexual melancholy is dealt with differently by the other guy—instead of internalizing or allegorizing it, he tends to externalize it and turn it into a kind of prideful suffering, while simultaneously using this outward acknowledgment as a false sense of gender progressiveness. And, third, 'friendly,' 'harmless' homophobic humor—so omnipresent in the world of the other guy (and Apatow films)—functions as a tacit acknowledgment (while also often begrudgingly being identified as an uncontrollable subconscious lack or failing) that something went wrong long ago with their fathers (or other, more symbolic male developmental relationships) and that, through the mutually imbricated actions of 'harmless' homophobia and 'bromantic' attachment, the other guy is admitting that the ubiquitous melancholia and its subsequent allegories are symptomatic of *something*, but that which cannot be named, for to name it is to risk self-conceit and concede duplicity. Whether this is a type of progress is unclear, particularly when one accounts for the obsessive desire of the Apatow crew (Rogen, Hill, Rudd, etc.) to fuse their personas—the everyday performativity of the male as well as the PR persona and on-screen characters—in an attempt to achieve a kind of seamless, authentic masculine continuum, which in turn could be read as an exceptionally elaborate allegorical exercise in personal grief counseling.

Returning to *Knocked Up*, the two central characters, Ben Stone (Seth Rogen) and Alison Scott (Katherine Heigl) serve as opposite poles of what Gen X/Yers see as post-collegiate life. He is a lazy stoner, living off a lawsuit settlement earned after he was hit by a car as a teenager, semi-working on a website that features information and time-stamps regarding when and where celebrities show up nude in their films, an idea that the guys seem to think is revolutionary, part of subverting the now co-opted, sold-out internet. As Gary Cross writes, "Advertising and consumer culture more broadly turned youthful rebellion into a commodity that wouldn't change even as boomers aged. Even the 'threat' of feminism could be reduced to (male) consumer desire."[17] And so these men literalize their distaste for feminism and their fetishizing of the female body into a form of rebellion, albeit one firmly and problematically lodged in the entertainment industrial complex. Alison, on the other hand, is a television producer for E! (an actual entertainment and celebrity-based cable TV channel), and we first see her at work as she haggles with Ryan Seacrest (playing himself, of course) after a promotion spot for one of Seacrest's myriad productions. Seacrest even complains about the 'haters' and that he currently has five jobs, self-cementing (while sending up) his reputation as the hardest working guy in Hollywood with a Napoleon complex. While Ben engages in a stoned-out American Gladiators tournament in his and his roommates' ramshackle backyard, Alison is brought into her boss' office and informed that they want her to step "in front of the camera." However, her boss and his assistant want her to "tighten it up," i.e., lose weight, poking fun at Hollywood's ludicrous body standards as well as its history of demeaning female actors (or 'talent' in general). Ben and Alison (I use his name first as the film focuses on his 'plight' during the pregnancy more thoroughly than on Alison's) first meet at a nightclub, he with his friends, and she with her friend Debbie (Leslie Mann), married to Pete (Paul Rudd), the future stars and central characters in *This Is 40*. Through casual sincerity, Ben manages to strike up a conversation with the much prettier Alison (he even says, "You're way prettier than I am," and as one of his buddies says, in a weirdly vicarious-transitive statement, "If a goofy guy like you had sex with her, I feel I had sex with her."), a rallying cry amongst all other guys, mirroring the plethora of TV and internet commercials where the pretty, slim wife is fed up with her clueless, slob of a husband (I deal with this conundrum later, in Chapter 4). Of course, we are treated (subjected?) to the awkward sex scene after he goes home with her, as well as the moment of ultimate other guy slackdom—he tries in vain to put on the condom, but in a moment of 'misunderstanding,' he conveniently 'hears' her say to not worry about it, "Just do it," to her means 'just put it (the condom) on.' To him, it means, 'just stick it in me.' This disjoint is essential to understanding the other guy—he is 'responsible' enough to have a condom, but, in the end, hears what he wants to hear when it comes to sex, so that while consent isn't an issue, contraception becomes something that is just too much work. Avoiding a small amount of work now is key, what comes next is, like much of his life, up in the air, not quite up to him, a marker of his conception of his waning power in both cultural and personal spheres. When they wake in the morning, she is mildly disgusted by him and her choice, yet is up and ready to go to work, while he lazily snores, oblivious until she pokes him awake. On the way out (the 'walk of shame') they pass Pete (Rudd; she lives in the family's backhouse, so while employed, she's not quite totally self-sufficient), who says, "Ah, to be young," in a mix of honest jealousy and dry disregard, setting up his character for the rest of this film and *This Is 40*.

After a microscopic shot of a cell dividing—emphasizing the bio-industrial, consumer-science that is 21st-century pregnancy—and several episodes of Alison with morning sickness, she and Debbie buy and use a dozen pregnancy tests, all with positive results. This leads her to a series of embarrassing and demeaning visits to gynecologists, one of which includes a trans-vaginal wand, a device lodged in America's brains after the Congressional and Senatorial misogynistic bullshit batted around during the lead up to the 2012 presidential election. Debbie and Pete, who already have two daughters (Apatow's real-life children), are supportive of her choice to have a child. However, there is no moment—not even a mention from any of the characters from her side of the narrative—where abortion is discussed, even as an option, something that Apatow seems to refuse to address, whether through studio pressure or personal choice (choice!). In a country where women's reproductive rights are consistently chipped away despite the decades since *Roe v. Wade*, this seems remiss at the least, irresponsible at the most. Apatow and his crew seem to be comfortable enough to deal with nearly every other hot button issue—race, gender, sexuality, age—as well as comfortable diving headfirst into gross-out shit-and-piss humor. But abortion seems to be out of the question, against the law, as it were. Additionally, Ben and his friends can only refer to it as the "A word," yet even this is comprised of all but two lines of dialogue, which seems particularly odd, since this is the male and his friends and Ben certainly wouldn't have to undergo the procedure. In fact, his friends see the pregnancy as something largely positive (other than Jonah Hill's character, who is the first to bring up the "A word," which makes sense in relation to Hill's characters in the films as well as his off-screen persona, often referred to in the popular press as vitriolic, moody and a bit of a 'dick'[18]), "I think it's great that you're gonna have a kid. Think of it this way, it's just an excuse to play with all your old toys again," one of his buddies quips. So, while Alison sees the pregnancy as a life-changing decision, Ben is thoroughly freaked out, and his friends see it as yet another chance to play. Welcome to the new great divide.

At a dinner where Ben and Alison discuss what they each want, Ben trots out his usual half-hearted reactions to everything, saying, "Whatever you wanna do, I'm gonna do. I'm on board," adding with sarcastic resignation, "Yay." Of course we know this is dishonest at best, as at dinner he is eating shrimp cocktail, something pregnant women are strongly encouraged to avoid. A montage follows, where they visit a baby store and a bookstore to look at child-rearing books, eventually sheepishly holding hands towards the end of the 'date.' Playing at romance, it seems, is something they've seen on TV or in film, the natural reaction to having a baby, or at least the bourgeois solution to most relationship crises (recall the commercials for Cialis™).

Pete and Debbie cement this when their daughters find out Aunt Alison is pregnant and ask questions; "Because people who love each other get married and have babies," coos Debbie, clearly unhappy in her problematic marriage to an other guy. But, it turns out, Ben is great with their kids and develops a keen bromance with Pete, born out of Pete's feelings of emasculation and domestic frustration and Ben's feelings of anxiety and confusion. Pete tells Ben to, "make an honest woman out of her," an almost anachronistically old-fashioned statement. What a comment like this does is, in a sense, make a 'whore' out of Alison (dishonest women get pregnant out of wedlock) while it admonishes Ben to step up and 'be a man.' This conservative 'logic' becomes all the more significant when later we find out that Alison was pregnant before she and Pete were married, a lynchpin that both Pete and Alison return to during arguments about their mess of a marriage (which really is just an overly familiar example of the effervescent suburban malaise that accompanies so much of consumer culture and its malcontents). During a conversation, Pete mentions that, "Isn't it weird that when you have a kid all your dreams and hopes go right out the window?" Regardless, Ben is going to do the 'right thing,' yet getting there is a process for Ben the other guy, whereas a 'real man' would presumably 'know' this, as it is an extension of conceptions of male domination and self-sufficiency. Yet, it's *force majeure* that opens Alison's eyes to just who Ben is when a literal earthquake strikes while the two are in bed together and Ben grabs his bong and ignores Alison. Concurrently, Debbie follows Pete to one of his 'meetings with a client' and finds him in a secretive, yet hilarious suburban paraspace, a fantasy football league meeting with his male friends.[19] She is appalled, feeling that she has 'cheated' on him, and so both of these debacles serve as plot devices to send Ben and Pete to Las Vegas for a night of male debauchery (standard practice for other guys in the face of domestic catastrophes, emblematized in the film *Swingers*).[20] While in Vegas, the boys visit a strip club (*de rigueur* for bromances), take psychedelic mushrooms and then attend a Cirque du Soleil performance in an often hilarious and warped version of the 'boys night out' (Apatow manages to make a Cirque show look even more grotesque than normal). The following exchange occurs while both are tripping on mushrooms in their hotel room:

Ben: Think they'll take us back?

Pete: Yes. But I don't know why. Do you ever wonder how someone could even *like* you?

> Ben: All the time, man, like, everyday. I wonder how *you* like me!

> Pete: How could Debbie like me? She likes me. She *loves* me. The big problem in our marriage is that she wants me around. She loves me so much that she wants me around *all the time*. That's our biggest problem!? And I can't accept that!? Like, that upsets me?

At the heart of this exchange is a type of male insecurity that is not often explored on screen, particularly in big budget Hollywood movies. If you caught yourself sympathizing with either character, that's part of the devious seductions of the other guy, a subtle victimization that is often cloaked in language that emphasizes that their *effort* is what counts. And here we also see a frisson at the heart of the male-female relationship—proximity. While the female is penciled in here as the needy, but true-hearted partner, the male is still the singular individual, as if Pete's inner Man with No Name is a persona he knows is a *problem*, but still he can't seem to keep him under wraps. At the heart of the other guy, again, is a conflict between not just the vibrant young man and the beaten middle-age man, but between his father—the remote, stoic Boomer—and the son—the wimpy, emotive Gen Xer. As Gary Cross writes in *Men to Boys: The Making of Modern Maturity*, "In modern times, each generation seems to define itself by the stories it embraces and the stories it rejects. As my generation broke away from our fathers, we, too, wanted new fantasies, and in the process of creating them we rebuffed old models of male maturation."[21]

After the two men return, the 'dark days' sequence follows, the boy-loses-girl segment of the narrative and plot. We see Ben growing up; he rents his own apartment, finds a job and shops for the baby, or as John Alberti writes in his excellent article on masculinity in the bromance film genre:

> Towards the end of the movie, the narrative momentum of the plot tries to revive the dialectical resolution of the bifurcated male hero as Ben begins to adopt—impersonate might be an even more resonant word—the trappings of Pete's more conventional gender roles of husband and father, landing a "real" job and moving into an adult apartment while Allison warms to the idea of having a father figure in her child's life.[22]

Alison does yoga, continues to work and preps a room in Pete and Debbie's house for the baby. When the big day arrives, Alison calls her gynecologist (a male that promised he would be available), but he is, alas, at a Bar Mitzvah out of town (a general commentary on men, but also another reference to Jewish masculinity, a trope that hits full speed in *This Is 40*), and so she calls Ben who rushes over, only to find her in a 'relaxation' bath, depicting her as adhering to the latest trends in birthing (a stressful delivery creates a stressful baby). Upon reaching the hospital, the camera focuses on Ben overcoming a series of challenges that enunciate his new-found maturity and manhood, although Alison is the one actually doing the labor. In particular, the latest doctor shows up and is a bit of a bully to Alison, to which Ben takes him aside, sternly speaks to him and gets re-sults. This tells us that when men bond, really see eye-to-eye, things in the world get done, even for the other guy. Ben also tells Debbie (who at this point thinks she will be the one in the delivery room with her sister) that he will be present and that she needs to leave, to which Debbie retorts (to Pete), "I think he's going to be a good dad. I think I like him," responding to his forceful, macho handling of the conflict as inherently authentic masculine behavior.

Again, Alberti writes;

> Ben even takes on aspects of the Alpha male, demanding that the male obstetrician treat Allison with more care and sensitivity. The birth of the baby functions magical-ly not so much to resolve the plot as to suggest that the further progress (if that's the right word) of the relationships under examination are a kind of *fait accompli*. Caught up in the moment, Debbie even suggests a longing for another child, an idea that scares Pete but that also ominously points to the inefficacy of assuming that parent-hood will automatically create a lasting bond between the characters. Ultimately, the question posed by Pete in that Las Vegas hotel room—"How can Debbie like me?" is never answered and haunts the movie's conclusion as well as the utopian possibilities of the bifurcated male hero.

The audience is also left with a final message: A provider goes out into the world and fights for his family, which also functions as a subtle stab at Pete's kind, yet passive other guy-ness, a rubric that, as Alberti writes, Ben is all too happy to mimic, implying that Ben sees Pete's other guy as a masculinity to which one aspires, a natural progression for him and his masculinity. To com-plete this locus, Ben's slacker friends populate the waiting room, his surrogate family still waiting around, representing the bulk of men at that age, the Lost Boys waiting to grow up, unwilling to leave Neverland. And, as with many Apatow films, the baby is a girl, yet another confusing Other to complicate the already overwhelmed other guy's previously carefree life, and a specter of what's to come in *This Is 40*.

Growing Up and Falling Apart: *This Is 40*

During an interview in *Rolling Stone*, Apatow spoke about what kinds of characters populate his world, particularly what kinds of character arcs work for audiences (or at least what appear to be arcs); "In hindsight, I've learned the audience will go along with a character so long as he is capable of handling his business."[23] What counts here is Apatow's use of the male pronoun (he wasn't asked to speak specifically about male characters), and how virile his characters would ostensibly appear, by handling "their business." Also useful here (and I'm not advocating for some version of auteur theory) is how Apatow sees his characters and their relative lack of growth within each film, particularly what Alberti calls the "bifurcated male hero." Caught between the Alpha and Beta masculine positions, these characters reflect a similar situation in the real, where the exigencies of political correctness and feminism are seen as emasculating, yet necessary to follow for masculine success in contemporary relationships with contemporary women (and men). Referring to *This Is 40* as a spin-off of *Knocked Up*, Apatow shows a potentially mature and complex approach to masculinity and the "bifurcated male" romantic hero, or as I have called them above, the alt-hero. However, Apatow also invests deeply into the central female character (Leslie Mann, playing the same Debbie from *Knocked Up*) and her struggles with her other guy husband (Paul Rudd playing Pete again). Now, this film is certainly not on par with Richard Linklater's intricate, unflinching *Before Sunrise/Sunset/Midnight* trilogy, but one can see that Apatow, now the age of his protagonists, has created characters, a setting and a problem that prove to be a deeper, more mature representation of men caught in the middle. However, the Woody Allenesque elements are still mired in a consumerist swamp, to the extent that we see BMWs in loving profile shots, visit the Coffee Bean and Tea Leaf café, and watch everyone in the household own and use an iPhone, iMac and/or iPad. So, this film, like its predecessor, is very much a middle-class, white film for straight people (with families), to the extent that both parents are forced to work (at, it should be mentioned, personally invested, 'cool' jobs) and face money problems because of the recession. This is an important distinction, as a key to romantic comedy writing 101 is that the characters never *need* money, nor seem to work more than 10 hours a week at their 'cool' job—fashion, wedding planning, dotcoms, music and entertainment, etc., or at an 'important' job—medicine, law, business, NPOs, etc. Money itself—and access to it—is what often enables most romantic comedic plots, while labor is seen as unromantic, dirty and a necessary evil (unless, again, it is the kind of work that is part of a hip or romantic identity package). The type of work is nearly as important as the brand of coffee maker or coffee table. And, so Pete works at a fledgling record label, still in love with the music and the musicians who make authentic rock and roll. Debbie owns and runs a women's boutique that offers clothing and accessories. So, the division of labor here is pretty obvious; Pete is allowed to still chase a dream that is heavily romanticized in the film (regardless if its failing, which it is), while Debbie is relegated to retail, blandly involved, but largely unvested throughout the story in a store that she owns and operates (and where an employee has been embezzling). They both sell stuff, but his is a cause, hers is a curse. That's what women get for venturing into the public sphere, the land of men.

We're treated to an illustration of their marriage, now five years later, when we see them having sex in the shower, and she hears him mention how great Viagra™ is. "We are young people. We don't need medication to have sex," Debbie screams, explaining that if he can't get an erection *because of her*, then the erection is a phony. The conversation then turns to his upcoming birthday and the party they are throwing, as well as the fact that she is turning 40 and how this needs to be ignored, or cursed. "I am not 40! Fuck 40! 40 can suck my dick!" she screams, to nobody in particular. So, with the use of the possessive, Debbie possesses a phallic power in the relationship that has become further articulated in relation to *Knocked Up*, and in fact, most of the film revolves around her anger issues, particularly in relation to Pete's other-guy indecisiveness. Debbie tends to police his eating (for health issues, instead of weight), yet has an entire smoking outfit so that she doesn't smell of smoke, for her children presumably, but also to deny Pete any ammunition in the relationship wars. Pete depicts the relationship as a constant battle; "We're in one of those phases where everything the other person says annoys the shit out of each other. All the time. It's a blast," even going as far as (with another married friend) imagining ways that Debbie might die (of course, in other-guy form, she passes away over a long period so that he can take care of her). While Pete spends long periods sitting on the toilet, playing Words with Friends on his iPad, Debbie asks, "Why is your instinct to escape?" And while a good deal of this is supposed to be funny, the film is often more acerbic and bitter, intimating a more mature vision of the romantic comedy, to the extent that *This Is 40* often feels more like a domestic 'dramedy' or melodrama. Even the usually buoyant Pete begins to feel besieged by the women in the house. "Sometimes I wish just one of you had a dick," Pete says, to which his youngest daughter replies, "Well, we don't want one," in relation to a disagreement be-tween listening to the Viking-grunge rock of Alice in Chains as opposed to the techno-dance pop of Lady Gaga. And escape he does, straight to work, where he is fighting a losing battle to make rocker Graham Parker relevant again to the under-30 crowd. Yet, at work, his attitude is utopian, as opposed to the emasculation he feels as home. The film also works hard at establishing an es-sentialist doctrine of gender as body discourse, with the various differences be-tween male and female bodies operating as the true barriers to communication and understanding. During a health montage, she gets a breast exam, while he has a cardiac test, regardless of the fact that the rate of cardiovascular disease in women is on the rise, while breast cancer is in decline in the U.S. This is compounded with discourses of age, as Pete's father (Albert Brooks, featuring his usual hyperbolic and funny kvetching) has married a younger woman (she is 45, he is 60) who has recently had triplets through fertilization aids. He is overwhelmed, at his age, with their energy and needs (he can't really tell the triplets apart, either). Similarly, Debbie's estranged father (John Lithgow, as demure as ever, an intellectualized pre-cursor to the other guy) has another family, including children the same ages as Pete and Debbie's. Pete and Deb-bie can't seem to connect with their parents, and they are quickly becoming too old to communicate with their kids (at least the way they would like to, as hip parents/friends), even trying to enforce a 'no digital devices' rule. The kids revolt in a scene that seems at odds with the technologized reality of the film, as the older daughter asks how she will do her homework with the new rule.

The bulk of the rest of the film (which critics overwhelmingly found to be overlong at 133 minutes, a good 30 minutes longer than the standard romcom) features a series of conflicts between Pete and Debbie, their kids, their parents and their own disappointments and frustrations, including Debbie's unplanned pregnancy. The final act also includes a number of tan-trums from Pete and Debbie (he crams cheeseburgers into his mouth, she flirts with a professional hockey player at a bar) that eventually drive them back together. In a monumentally self-absorbed moment of insular logic, they ask, "Why do people keep attacking us? The truth is, this isn't about us. It's about our parents," illustrating not only the self-congratulatory logics of much of pop psychology, but also a middle-class tone of vilified victimhood. In many ways, Debbie continues to be positioned as the male in the relationship, again referring to her own body featuring male sex organs; "I can't believe I've wast-ed my whole life busting the balls of people who have no balls. I'm the only one that has balls!" Reaching back to films such as *Rebel Without a Cause* and the cultural anxieties over 'mama's boys' in post-WWII America—men raised by their mothers while their fathers were off fighting for God and country—we are again faced with the emasculating force of the Mother in the domestic. Yet here, instead of a son, it is Pete who runs the risk of infantilization and symbolic castration, the other guy as mama's boy, tamed husband, failed businessman, and flummoxed father. Pete's father even goes so far as to say to Debbie, "Pete's never been a fighter. That's why he married you. You're the fighter." And, yet, the film never feels as if it's excusing either Debbie or Pete's behaviors, content instead to illustrate how, with new and alternate forms of identity (and particularly masculinity) the domestic space has become naturally destabilized. Is Pete to blame? When all of it comes to a head, he predictably speeds off on his bicycle (Apatow seems to have a predilection for men who ride bikes, particularly during film climaxes), eventually hitting an open car door, and being punched by an older, tougher guy, who says, "It's not my job to look out for you. You look out for yourself. Don't disrespect me." I turn again to Alberti's probing work;

> *Knocked Up* directly engages the question of the long term viability of these alternate forms of masculinity by juxtaposing the pre-marriage romance of Ben and Alison with the post-romantic trials of Pete and Debbie, trials that underscore both Apatow's anxiety over the possible obsolescence of conventional constructions of masculinity within the logic of the romantic comedy and the dubious viability of the various bromantic experimental alternatives of the bifurcated male pairs that define the subgenre. In this way, the Apatow bromances contain a logic of generic self-consciousness and self-critique that belies readings of them as simply reactionary or regressive.[24]

Here, Alberti argues for the value of these films, as well as more bromantic films such as *I Love You, Man*, particularly as cultural markers of shifts in the depth and complexity present in the acknowledgment of gender instabilities. When considering these films within the larger U.S. film-production system, it's obvious yet important to note that Hollywood isn't so much selling US ideology as it is assuring its imperialistic control of the global film market with its catch-all demographic appeal blockbusters and mutually assured (and understood) catastrophe films. However, I would argue, as Alberti does, that the romantic comedy as well as its offshoots, including mumblecore and bromances, offer a few radical surprises, particularly in their exploration of the various permutations of the other guy, the alt-hero and the Apatow crew of masculine misfits, stoners and authentic everyman movie stars. Additionally, it's the women that make these films (Lena Dunham, for instance) and that feature in them that is often interested in what the other guy looks and feels like, for at least this kind of masculinity is less likely to shoot bad guys and beat up women, instead using self-reflection, emotions and words as a means of fumbling toward some semblance of progressive masculine subjectivity.

In the next chapter, I inspect sitcoms, both more traditionally male-driven examples as well as the new other-guy-centered sitcoms, where the fight between work and leisure, public and domestic space plays out in the structurally closed manner of both the multi-camera sitcom narrative structures, as well as in the more dynamic, reality-TV-based single camera shows. In both of these types, the other guy remains a central figure, particularly (as in both mumblecore and Apatow films) due to his ability to operate as a foil for more traditional, macho types, as well as a confused, but sweet-natured guy we root for, even as he fumbles his way toward a masculinity he can be proud of.

Notes

1. A Generation Finds Its Mumble, Dennis Lim, Aug 19, 2007, *New York Times* online.
2. Maria San *Filippo*, *Cineaction* 85, 2011.
3. Filippo.
4. Filippo.
5. Filippo.
6. Interview with the Duplass Brothers, Tiny Mix Tapes.com, Alex Peterson, July 2012.
7. Gary Cross, *Men to Boys: The Making of Modern Immaturity*, (New York: Columbia University Press, 2008), 148–149.
8. Deborah S. David and Robert Brannon, *The Forty-Nine Percent Majority: The Male Sex Role*, (New York: Addison-Wesley, 1976).
9. Tamar Jeffers McDonald, "Homme-Com: Engendering Change in Contemporary Romantic Comedies," in *Falling in Love Again: Romantic Comedy in Contemporary Cinema*, eds., Stacey Abbott and Deborah Jermyn (London: I.B. Taurus & Co, 2009), 158.
10. Jeffers McDonald, 158–159.
11. John Alberti, "I Love You, Man: Bromances, the Construction of Masculinity and the Continuing Evolution of the Romantic Comedy," *Quarterly Review of Film and Video*, #30, 159–172, 2013, p. 160.
12. Alberti, 160.
13. Barry Keith Grant, *Shadows of Doubt: Negotiations of Masculinity in American Genre Films*, (Detroit: Wayne State U. Press, 2011), 11.
14. Grant, 5.
15. One such bit from the film, "You know how I know you're gay?" has become an internet meme, where thousands of user-generated shorts featured on YouTube and other online

video sources attempt to outdo one another in a race to signify what straight men consider 'gay' behavior or norms.

16. Judith Butler, *Gender Trouble: Feminism and the Subversion of Identity*, (New York: Routledge, 1990), 179.

17. Gary Cross, *Men to Boys*, 147.

18. *Rolling Stone* interview on *This Is the End*.

19. Fantasy football, where players select their 'ultimate' team roster from actual NFL players and see whose team finishes the season with the most points, is a prevalent trope (the game itself and it as male retreat) throughout other guy land, to the extent that an entire sitcom, *The League*, is devoted to how men play and use the game as a means to escape work, family and women (and sometimes male romantic partners).

20. I use the term 'catastrophe' in the Greek dramatic sense, a 'downturn' in the action, but also perhaps the moments where the chorus on stage turned from the protagonist to the audience. In rom-coms, particularly Apatow's, domestic catastrophes serve as plot devices where the male characters can effectively 'turn' to the audience and, with a wink, show them that they are 'real guys,' while including the audience in their own pratfalls. *The Hangover* film series effectively uses this technique—nearly breaking the 4th wall—a structural and formulaic tool as exegesis and plot driver.

21. Gary Cross, *Men to Boys: The Making of Modern Maturity*, (New York: Columbia U. Press, 2008), 148.

22. John Alberti, "'I Love You, Man': Bromances, the Construction of Masculinity and the Continuing Evolution of the Romantic Comedy," *Quarterly Review of Film* and Video, #30, 2013, 159–172, 165.

23. Interview with Judd Apatow, *Rolling Stone* #1192, Sept. 26, 2013, 63.

24. Alberti, 170–171.

· 3 ·

"I FEEL HEARD AND VALIDATED"

The Other Guy and Sitcoms

Truth number one:
I don't want to talk about it.
I want to figure it out.

Truth number two:
When you ask me what's on my mind and I say "nothing,"
I really mean nothing.

From 36.5 *Truths About Men*
womenshealthmag.com

In the pilot episode of the sitcom *Perfect Couples* (NBC, 2011), the action begins with three separate scenes, one at each of the 20/30-something couples' houses, all featuring a splayed out wife on the bed and a husband trying to figure out how to get into bed without disturbing their sleeping mate. The answer is in their reactions. The first guy, Dave, is flabbergasted and confused with Julia (his wife) at first, settling into a silent tantrum; the second guy, Vance, mixes frustration and mild disgust (presumably at the situation but also at his wife, Amy, who wears a tank top and running shorts, laying spread-eagle on her stomach); the third guy, Rex, is generally flummoxed with Leigh, his wife, scratching himself and gesticulating nervously before the camera pans to a past-the-body shot of a book on the nightstand, *Communication for*

Couples,'written' by a male, 'Brandon Grace.' This piece of *mise en scène* is telling. 'Grace' points to the body, intimating poise and elegance, whereas the first name, 'Brandon,' works as a 'sensitive guy' name with similar class repercussions, as if only upper-middle-class white men have the capacity for sensitivity and communication with women. I draw attention to this seemingly inconsequential detail as the entirety of the one and only season of *Perfect Couples* is incredibly carefully staged, with many visual and aural 'easter eggs' in each episode. In this sense, the show mirrors the other guy's attention to detail in designing and maintaining the home, and the similar way he manages his physique, hobbies, friends and partners. Returning to the show, Rex flips through the book quickly, looking for a familiar passage, places the book down and recites the following with ritual diligence: "Cherished partner, I honor your need to be comfortable, yet when you leave me so little room, it makes me feel unloved." Leigh wakes upon hearing this declaration (never mind that he felt impelled to wake her up to in order to share this) and answers, "Cherished partner, now I know when I leave you so little room, you feel unloved." Each says this dutifully, in a rehearsed, automated manner. The next shots continue the hijinks, with Dave trying to gently roll Julia over using the sheets, while Vance and Amy, in a close up of both of their faces, Vance passive-aggressively talk-yelling at her that, "clearly your comfort is the only thing that matters. Please, take the other 5 percent, too! I'm just gonna sleep on the floor like a dog!" (It's interesting here to note that each of the three couples features a real dog, a man with a dog's name—Rex— and Vance referring to himself as a 'dog.') This turns into a full-fledged argument. Rex and Leigh are shown holding hands and professing to each other in a creepily sincere tone, "And by revealing our needs, we forge a bond, two becoming one." Each scene continues with more immature tactics. Vance and Amy devolve into a histrionic and nasty fight; Dave waggles a flashlight at their dog in the bedroom, causing him to bark, which then wakes her up, while he performatively reprimands the dog for waking Julia up. He then gives the dog a 'thumbs up,' the dog being his male 'buddy' as opposed to his wife (or any woman, most likely). Rex, speaking to no one in particular, "You're right about that book. I feel heard and validated," ending with him meekly trying to wedge his way onto the bed that his now asleep wife lies spread across. Vance and Amy passionately roll around on the floor kissing and groping each other in the stereotypical 'make-up sex' mode. A cool yet comic, upbeat blues progression plays over the entire opening segment, adding the requisite, quirky, absurdist edge found so often in contemporary sitcoms. The final scene ends with an exterior shot of Vance and Amy's house, the drapes open, them locked in an aggressive sex-wrestle. An older man walking his dog stops to watch as the title *Perfect Couples* slides onto the screen, framing two generations at odds. We watch him watch them, both of 'us' supposedly bewildered at the 21st-century minefield that is relationships, yet implicitly passive in our collective involvement in the production and representation of this odd, comic and sad dysfunction. Moving from out of the bedrooms, out onto the street and onto our couches as we watch this suburban malaise, we become voyeurs of their lives, nudge-nudging and wink-winking with our partners, smugly saying 'we aren't like that at all!' Or, more silently, painfully, asking ourselves, 'are we like that?' By ending with an exterior shot, the director/producers/writers involve the viewer, implicate the viewer and incriminate the viewer—you are these people, you let things get this bad, and you are the ones to blame. Particularly the men.

In addition to the bevy of new channels for men—ESQ Channel (from *Esquire* magazine[1]), Spike and FXX—and the reality shows targeting men who love cars (*Xtreme 4x4*, *Top Gear*, *Horsepower TV*, *Counting Cars*), travel (*Boundless*, *The Getaway*, *Man Shops Globe*), home improvement (*Flipping Out*, *Man Caves*), as well as the long-running videogame promotional/review show *X-Play* (not to forget LOGO, aimed primarily at gay men), a horde of new sitcoms aimed at men have aired during the second half of the economic crisis that has struck the U.S. (and the rest of the globe). These shows, and the sheer number of them, illustrate not only a general cultural concern for the relative 'fragility' of men, the potentially 'new normal' economic picture, the crisis of masculinity in general and their waning political and social power, but also how masculinities like the other guy have become a familiar brand of entertainment and ridicule. Shows that feature males as leads or an all-male principal cast like *We Are Men*, *Men at Work*, *Guys with Kids*, *The Millers*, *The Michael J. Fox Show*, *Sean Saves the World*, *Dads*, and *About a Boy* are certainly enunciating the zeit of the geist when it comes to men's issues, particularly the much-touted 'fall of men' and ongoing 'mancession.' In this chapter, I look closely at selected episodes from three sitcoms—*Last Man Standing*, *Man Up!* and *Men at Work*—as a means of tracing symptoms of current masculine crises, as well as in order to better flesh out the other guy and what makes him tick. The three selected shows and episodes also represent, in a certain sense, Raymond Williams' concepts *dominant*, *residual* and *emergent* as a means of theorizing the ways that masculinity, like culture, struggles to maintain balance, while aggregating power, in the face of dynamic social, political and economic change.[2] I finish with a short look at *Modern Family*, the critically acclaimed sitcom often cited as progressive in terms of topics like age, race, sexuality, gender and same-sex partnerships and families. However, as I will trace out below, a great deal of the American sitcom's appeal and longevity (in general) is in its ability to push acceptable social mores while remaining remarkably entrenched in more conservative forms and themes. Thus, the TV sitcom is an ideal media form to trace out further details of the other guy's synaesthetic masculinity and his transformation into a potentially progressive male representation, performance and self.

TV, Men, Sitcoms

It is obvious perhaps, but still important, to begin by stating that television and consumption are mutually imbricated and constitutive. From its beginning, TV has been a commercial medium, broadcast to enormous audiences, broken up into digestible bits of narrative, competition, drama and comedy by equally structured advertisements (not to mention the long history of product placement). In a similar sense, the wholesale commodification of daily life was both a product of TV as well as a commodity *sold* by TV itself. And so in the 1950s, alongside the drive-in theatre, the suburban mall, Googie architecture and demographic-driven advertising, the TV served as a unifying American experience, yet one that *seemed* to treat each viewer as essentially separate, and therefore, special. As brilliantly narrativized (and somehow documented) by the AMC series *Mad Men*, TV is a uniquely suited medium to engage men, women, and families in the domestic space, while promising the excitement of the movie theatre, the sports stadium, and the (upwardly) mobilized gaze from the naugahyde seats of the family car. And while the TV has often been theorized as a conceptually feminine device in terms of content (from soap operas to daytime talk shows) as well as ideology and utility (the 'feminine,' self-contained domestic sphere), I would also like to draw attention to TV as equally aimed at and tailored for men.[3] In fact, the birth of modern masculinity is often identified as occurring in the 1950s, particularly a central dialectic involving the rigidity of the loyal and regimented company man and the hip young attitude of the new consuming male, or what Michael Kimmel calls, "White collar conformists and suburban playboys."[4] TV programming and advertising quickly segmented men into distinct demographic categories based on race, class, geographic location, and other factors, and in doing so became a significant cultural driver of men's conceptions of themselves, a taste-maker *par excellence* while also managing to function as a place that reflected 'American values' that also sought to uphold conventions (depending on the genre, studio and advertising dollars). Interestingly, television studies and masculinity studies also grew up alongside each other (as did Cinema studies), both emergent fields charged by the postmodern turn as well as the cultural keystones of women's and minority rights, visibility and identity politics, and the codification of the goals of the New Left (amongst many other factors). Key figures in early television studies such as Stuart Hall, Raymond Williams, Dick Hebdige, John Fiske and John Hartley traced out key methods and approaches, from textual analysis of the programs themselves, to studies of TV as an institutional latticework, with political economies of scale and transnational audiences. As Charlotte Brunsdon writes, "This television, the television studied in television studies, is a production of the complex interplay of different histories—disciplinary, national, economic, technological, legislative—which not only did not exist until recently, but is currently, contestedly, being produced even as, simultaneously, the nationally regulated terrestrial broadcasting systems which are its primary referent move into convulsion."[5] Here, Brunsdon suggests that because of TV's inherently hybrid, distributed nature, the approaches to the study of TV themselves are in constant flux in addressing the medium itself. Contemporary digital technologies and their deployment are particularly perplexing—streaming, commercial-free 'televisual' shows on Netflix such as *House of Cards* (2013), webisode content on NBC.com, viewing practice variances on DVR-equipped screens (home digital recorders that allow the viewer to skip past commercials, for instance), or 'on demand' TV programming offered on commercial airplane flights are examples—and often require multi-disciplinary approaches. While it is not the aim of this study to track down the other guy across multiple TV genres or platforms, it is important to note that TV is consumed in a hybrid fashion, thus our engagement with representations of the other guy across TV is reflective and constitutive of the other guy's inherently contingent and polyvalent nature.

One key TV genre, the sitcom, has figured prominently as a means of representing both traditional masculine norms as well as more emergent, progressive forms of maleness, principally as staged in the domestic domain and at the job site. From *Cheers* (1982–93) to *Married...with Children* (1987–97), *Friends* (1994–2004) to *The Office* (2005–2013), these long-running and commercially successful U.S. sitcoms all featured men as central characters caught in maelstrom of historical and cultural change that contemporary masculinity and men have turned into a series of internal and external crises. Both *Cheers* and *Married…with Children* featured several different male types (the dim-witted bartender, Woody, or the oversexed son, Bud), so that the protagonist (Sam Malone, Al Bundy) would (as the genre so often demands) remain resistant to change, the heroic, hegemonic male sticking to his guns. *Friends* and *The Office* on the other hand, were ensemble comedies centered around male relationships and how these bonds often competed with female relationships. Rebecca Feasey, in *Masculinity and Popular Television*, writes that, "…the representation of male friendship, homosociality, and homosexuality are as important, if not more important than heterosexual relations in the contemporary sitcom."[6] She goes on to analyze episodes and scenes from *Friends*, *Coupling* (often referred to as the British *Friends*) and *Will & Grace*, finding that while, "…American and British sitcoms exploit dominant cultural ideologies regarding male friendship, it is worth noting the ways in which they also depict potentially empowering representations of male bonding and homosociality for the mainstream audience."[7] However, Feasey warns that the dictates of the genre itself prevent truly radical departure from accepted speech and behavior, as the politics of representation in the medium are so ideologically inhibited by its commercialized nature and configuration. Further, I would add that because of this contestation between commercial interests in male spending and consumption and the broadcast nature of network TV, the other guy is almost a *natural outgrowth* of this genre. This is true regardless of whether the shows are streamed or DVR'd because of the additional content that the other guy is always-already assumed to engage with (websites, trailers, webisodes, social media adverts and promotions, games and apps, etc.) while watching, using a second screen, or afterwards between broadcasts or viewings. Additionally, as I will discuss below, the development of the single-camera, reality-show based format (as used in *The Office* or *Modern Family*) provides a suitably familiar, ironic, fragmented and competitive dimension to viewing. These shows, formal attributes, taken from reality-TV proper, resemble videogame cut-scenes, and mirror—particularly the 'testimonials,' where characters speak directly to the camera (and, ostensibly, the producers)—the other guy's emotional 'need' to share, his gratification in being in-the-know about 'how things really work' in the media, his self-aware pride in being an active viewer, consumer and co-producer of TV texts and their connection to social media, the web, and the techno-*savoir faire* hierarchy that they and their male friends prop up and maintain.

The Real Man and Authenticity—Tim Allen

Three young white women sit around a kitchen table in a well-furnished and comfortable looking upper-middle-class home, making a banner that reads "Welcome Back Dad." Mom (Vanessa, played by Nancy Travis, who has played the kind and patient wife several times before on other sitcoms) sits just outside, reading a magazine and drinking a glass of white wine. Kristin, the eldest, has her son Boyd on her lap (she got pregnant in high school and is now a single mom, living with her parents and sisters, working as a server at a diner). Mandy and Eve snap at each other as sisters do. "Your dad's home," Vanessa says, getting up to greet him. Eve, the youngest and a tomboy says, "Oh, finally. I've been cooped up with you hens long enough." Vanessa: "Oh, Eve, honey, it's not cute when you're Dad says it, and it's just confusing when you do," portending the clear-cut gender identities in force and enforced in the household. "I'm back!" yells Mike Baxter as he walks in the front door, returning home after a long hunting and fishing trip, sponsored by his employer, Outdoor Man, an outdoor lifestyle store akin to Patagonia. He proudly plops a three-foot long fish on top of a banner designed by his three daughters that reads "Welcome home, dad." His wife asks, "What am I supposed to do with this?!" Mike: "You slice it. Mouth to anus. Pull every-thing out. Pretty self-explanatory. I'm gonna grab a shower," intimating that Vanessa does—must do—the cooking (she, in fact, along with a full-time job, seems to run the entire house, even after Mike scales back his work schedule when Vanessa takes a meaningful promotion). This is the set-up. Four women, one guy, Mike, battling for supremacy, railing against the social and political changes sweeping the nation, particularly when it comes to masculinity. At one point, Eve needs a ride to soccer. Mike responds, "Soccer—that's Europe's covert war for the hearts and minds of America's kids," and goes on to berate the sport further. Eve mentions that the "boys will be scrimmaging the girls," to which Mike responds, "Well, the boys aren't that tough. They run around, get hair gel in their eyes, run into the goal posts and cry." So, here Mike accomplishes several monolithic male heroics; he degrades his daughter's choice of sport (the fact that it's an un-American sport), and denigrates the men who choose to play it as effete and clearly not as tough as those that play the real American sports: football, baseball, and basketball. He says all of this to the one daughter that is the ostensible tomboy; she needs to be 'reigned in' for perhaps being not feminine enough? He is also unable to communi-cate with his middle daughter, Mandy, the 'fashionista,' social networker and popular girl at her school. As the series progresses, though, it becomes clear that for Mike's macho-man schtick to work, he must be faced with a host of stereotypical women; the tomboy, the 'girly-girl,' the fallen angel (his pre-adult daughter with her own daughter) and Vanessa, his wife, the professional woman who wants it all. In essence, the writers and producers have created a world where Mike is in constant conflict with women (all white women?), history and culture. Yet, at the end of nearly all episodes over the course of the three seasons aired thus far (a fourth season is in production at the time of this writing, with ratings still high for its time slot), Mike's masculinity is written and acted as what just 'makes good common sense.' His advice, as rejected as it is by the women in his life, reliably ends up saving the day. Mike is right because he follows his gut (and a rather protruding gut, at that). He's right because American white middle-class masculinity has always been 'right,' and will continue to be if, presumably, one is to trust that the show's creators and audience will be 'right' in perpetuity.

Last Man Standing is a multi-camera sitcom on ABC (first airing in the fall of 2011), featuring Tim Allen as Mike Baxter, a white, (late) middle-aged father of three married to a professional woman (a geologist and 'graduate of Ohio State University'). Mike works as the director of marketing for the "Outdoor Man" chain of sporting goods stores, a kind of far right, surly, jokester Don Draper. This is Tim Allen's second sitcom on ABC—the first being *Home Improvement*, a very successful, eight-season program that aired during the 1990s, centering on the Taylor family, a midwestern family run with macho aplomb by Allen's character, Tim. Needless to say, Allen as an actor, spokesperson and celebrity has found mass appeal as a 'real' American man, one who loves cars, his family, but most of all, power tools (his character on *Home Improvement* is actually the host of *Tool Time*, a show-within-a-show home improvement show). In fact, Allen, raised in Denver, Colorado, and in Birmingham, Michigan (a suburb of Detroit), started as a stand-up comic, his act focusing on masculinity and the foibles involved in trying to be a 'real' man. Of course, he studied theatre, communications, philosophy and design at universities in Michigan, and talks openly about his macho character as an 'act.' Yet, he has proven himself to be remarkably prescient and interminable in his portrayal of a particular type of midwestern masculinity, and Allen inhabits the male role on *Last Man Standing* in almost exactly the same manner as he did on *Home Improvement*—he is the last of a dying breed, a simple guy who loves his family and has grown weary of the new breed of 'men-as-wussies,' albeit over the course of more than two decades.[8]

Later in the pilot, Mike returns to work, a bustling, well-lit, clean and entirely male-staffed office/warehouse, one of the Outdoor Man chain of stores (clearly, Mike's manliness doesn't include a critique of 'big corporations' taking over the small towns of the U.S., illustrating just how complicated and inconsistent his regressive, 'authentic' masculinity plays out over the run of the series), saying, "Hey guys! It's great to be back in the sanctuary. No hair-dryers, no tears, no citrus body wash. Smells like balls in here." I love the utter strangeness of this line. Mike's workplace is a temple to Man, a "sanctuary" where no women may enter, where the smell of testicles makes him both proud and nostalgic. Men sit at brown, sturdy, wood desks polishing rifles, or walk the floor unpacking hiking boots and crossbows, carrying boxes with the Outdoor Man logo proudly emblazoned on the side. And while the delight-fully omnipresent erotics of homosociosensuality and male body-bonding on display here are foregrounded as straight male emphatic *straightness*, it seems as if Mike, the men in the office, the writers/producers and the audience have come to a point where the acknowledgment of this naughty undercurrent is best viewed and heard out in the open, as it were. So, by clearly mentioning "balls" and how happy the smell makes him, Mike is almost masochistically identifying the homoerotic as über-present, so present that he is an inch away from embracing it (or however many inches is considered long enough). So goes the latest form of straight male homophobia, deferral and denial. After Mike reminisces on the macho pleasure of sweaty ball smell, a young worker, Kyle, smiles, holding a box, and sniffs the air deeply, smiling appreciatively. Mike then looks at him with disdain, "Who are you?" Kyle, it turns out, is a near perfect other guy. He is kind, sincere, a little slow (but not dumb), blonde and cute. He's in his early 20s, has a job, but no real plan for life, and likes to bake. More on him in a moment.

Throughout the rest of the pilot and next two episodes, Mike ends up scal-ing back on his work so that his wife can take a promotion, further tumbling into the muddle of feminine domestic space. He counters this by taking to the internet to vlog about how men aren't men anymore; "What's happened to men?! Modern men, what do you do? You run from stuff—responsibility, fatherhood. You can't even change a tire!" These rants of course (in another interesting media-within-media-masculine-rant turn for Tim Allen) go viral, and so Mike finds a community that appreciates what he has to say. However, the show often 'turns up the juice' with his character, and then summarily dials it back when thorny social issues are tackled. Mike complains about his daughters always asking for money ("I'm not an ATM. You know how I know?

I only speak English," to which his youngest daughter—his stand-in for a son—high-fives him), and so encourages his middle daughter, Mandy, to get a job. She does, and in one of the many palpably sexist storylines the show seems to casually toss off, featuring each of the daughters and Vanessa, Mandy loses her first job at a boutique because she 'bought too many clothes with her employee discount.' He then gets her a job delivering pizzas, but at his wife's behest, Mike then stalks her while she drives around the neighborhood while she delivers pizzas, along with Kyle, the other guy (in Kyle's van, no less). While they tail Mandy's car, Mike reminisces, "When you're young, everything's possible. Even admitting you're wrong to a household filled with women." Mike just can't seem to figure it out. Poor guy. And, so yet again, we see evidence of the authentic, recalcitrant white middle-aged male on TV framed as the victim of his circumstances, but also of a changing world that won't accommodate his traditional and 'true' American ideals. Don Draper probably would have just *left* this family, like a real man. Finally, what stands out throughout *Last Man Standing* is that although Mike is the titular character, it's Kyle who proves to be remarkably consistent, particularly in his other-guy-ness. However, his character is written as a constant subordinate to Mike, ritualistically sacrificed on the comedy pyre in order to prop up Mike's fight to the death, against women, gays and lesbians, the youth, subcultures, people of color and any other non-normative subject or subjectivity that simultaneously allows him to play the victim and the holdout. Mike must perform the *Last Man Standing* as if he were an angel who's wings are caught up in a cold derecho of history, sweeping what was formerly good and right out of his reach, so that progress is always framed as an assault, on his body and his psyche. What then will become of America if men like him disappear?

Man Up!

If *Last Man Standing* is a testament to the imagined monolithic immutability of hegemonic masculinity, then *Man Up!* is an attempt to address the implied 'wussiness' of the other guy, to the point that the show both espouses a crisis of real masculinity, and offers a guidebook to address these issues. Yet, at heart, *Man Up!* is a wolf in sheep's clothing—particularly since the men in the show are spectacular fuck ups in their attempts to, literally, Man Up (a subterranean ode to the videogame logic of 'leveling up,' where the player completes one level of the game and moves onto the next). Advertisements on ABC (aired during breaks from *Last Man Standing*) feature the following tagline: "They won't grow up, can't measure up, and they're always screwing up," expressing their regressive boyhood status, their physical lack (penis and otherwise) and their inability to learn the new rules of maledom. (Videogame logics permeate this show, as well as others, signaling just how central games and play are to men's navigation of the new gender schematics). Airing on ABC from October 18 to December 6, 2011, only eight episodes aired because of low ratings, with the other five available online for one month.

The premiere episode begins with the three central characters playing a multiplayer online war-themed videogame, something like *Call of Duty*, with each barking instructions and orders to each other over wireless headsets, black controllers in their hands. We see each from a straight-on camera angle, so that they are staring directly into the camera, and presumably, our households. When filming scenes with a single camera, the angle that is closest to 0 degrees (or looking straight at the subjects) is meant to signify a great personal intimacy, while angles that move to either side become progressively less intimate as they angle away from the character's direct sightline. This is significant for several reasons. First, we viewers are posed as inside the game, and although we clearly are not in their game, the world they are looking into and playing in is *our* world—so that the 'world of us' is in fact a kind of videogame for them, where it's important for them to play and win like real men. Second, our first introduction to all three characters is both intimate and disconcerting to the extent that they appear to be shouting and staring directly at us, the viewer, implying their exposed nature as other guys, and as a kind of scientific subject, an oddity that we observe in their natural habitat. And yet this also marks them as evolutionarily obtuse, outside of the familiar realm of normative white, male behavior. Additionally, their distinct personality types are writ large through their playing styles: Will (played by Mather Zickel) is the almost-alpha male, married with kids, leading the charge, but lacking in the requisite absolute certainty of true macho-ness; Kenny (Dan Fogler) is the overweight, bearded, divorced, foul-mouthed slob (really, here Fogler is blatantly rehashing the work of actor/comedian Jack Black, a good candidate for the hyper-obnoxious proto-other guy) who plays with an ultra-violent streak; and Craig (Christopher Moynihan, also creator of the show), the loveable, wimpy, skinny friend who gamefully follows the other two. Ending in a flurry of gunfire, the three revel in their victory (against, presumably, another three-man team of online gamers) with Will asking, "Who's the man?" and Kenny and Henry yelling, "You're the man!" back to Will, while Will (completing the cycle) yells, "I am the Man!" to himself, his friends and the world in general. Here we have a mixture of hero-worship, homosocial 'circle jerk,' and masturbatory congratulation, all safely regulated by the distance afforded by the game, and yet staged in a genre of games where boys and men bond together to cooperatively kick ass and virtually dominate. This scene is of course capped by the ultimate heteronormative, psycho-social authority—Will's wife, Theresa (Teri Polo, who seems to play the kind and loving wife as much as Nancy Travis does) who yells, "Will, the kids are sleeping!" The guys, as if scolded by their mother, whisper the same 'you the man' statements. We then see the title card, black letters and a red 'U' festooned with an arrow pointing up.

It bears noting how each dude's couch/domicile has been designed, as the camera continues to frame each from the same angle for the remainder of the scenes, with a just slightly wider frame. Will is in a clearly middle-class home, sitting on a couch covered with toys and laundry (at one point he pulls a Barbie from under his butt), Kenny's space features a stand-up, arcade videogame, take-out soda cups and various fanboy ephemera on primitive shelving, while Craig's place is tastefully furnished and an acoustic guitar sits next to him, presumably for him to play while he gently woos his romantic interests. The *mise en scène* here is significant, as the other guy is entirely obsessed with stuff—toys, collectibles, clothes, games, junk—anything that serves as a performative and self-conscious signifier of his interests and identity. This is partially due to the overwhelming embrace of commodity culture that other guys perform as inimitably ironic, and partially due to the collection instinct they seem to have. This is akin to Walter Benjamin's theorization of collecting in "Unpacking My Library." In this mild deviation from his more strident, Marxist work, Benjamin finds that the collector is in many ways reigniting a childlike mythos in order to construct a system that enables them to understand their toys and belongings by giving them a fetishistic quality. Collectors, he writes, "accomplish renewal of existence [through] the while range of childlike modes of acquisition, from touching things to giving them names."[9] In this sense, the other guy buys and displays objects as a means of revisiting a lost childhood that he feels he should still have, indeed one that he deserves. The collector has "a relationship to objects that does not emphasize their functional, utilitarian value—that is their usefulness."[10] This materialist historicity is alive and well in the other guy, with an important caveat; while the act of purchasing is partially superseded by the act of owning, what is most vital is the object's relationship to the other objects on display. To collect only one kind of thing is seen as obsessive, too far into the realm of either women's more traditional collecting of, say, figurines, or men's collecting of action figures (the actions of a 'true geek'), but to collect a wide variety of objects signifies a kind of kitsch literacy, a pop cultural know-how.

Continuing with the episode at hand, the next scene is shot in Will and Theresa's kitchen during a quotidian middle-class morning, where the household is preparing for work and school. Theresa is, strangely, not going to work, a fairly substantial anachronism for the new masculine sitcom. She is, instead, preparing lunches for the kids when she asks Will to open a small package (a task she is surely able to do). It ends up being a new videogame that Will mistakes as for himself (she actually bought if for their son's birthday). This leads to Will mentioning that the game is rated 17+, where their son is no more than 12, a fact that is glossed over quickly. This says much about the men of the house—what counts is that the son is engaging in violent play, damn the ratings. Will also worries about what to get his son for his birthday that will sufficiently mark his transition from boyhood to manhood, when Theresa calls out Will for his lack of 'manliness.' Will protests, to which Theresa replies, "Your grandfather fought in WWII, your father fought in Vietnam, but you play videogames and use pomegranate body wash." Will responds, "Are you saying I'm not a man?" "You are man-ish," Theresa replies. Here we see the pervasive policing effect, so that women in this world add further anxiety to the other guy's at-risk masculinity, placing Theresa in the role of the bitch, the mother and the nag. We also have fighting and nationalism as the key markers for masculine action and self-worth, to the extent that violent videogames, even though arguably far too violent for their son's age, are configured as a means for the son to explore his masculinity, but not Will. He's too old. At this game, he just can't win.

The always keyed-up Kenny appears in the kitchen, has a mini-row with his ex-wife, Brenda (Theresa's sister), who also happens to be there, and Will exhorts Kenny to 'play it cool.' Kenny identifies Tobey Maguire as his go-to cool guy (a kind-hearted other guy in his acting roles if ever there was one, and Spiderman to boot—the superhero *hiding out* as other guy). As incongruous as this seems, one gets the sense that this is meant as a zinger, but it falls flat because Kenny's masculine neuroticism doesn't match his choice of hero, nor does it match his character (a major failing of the show, so much so that each character undergoes several major character changes over the course of the aired episodes, to the extent that it feels like an exercise in demographic and fan-based manipulation for audience share). A short work scene follows where nobody does any work (Will is an insurance salesman—another potential Willy Loman). Instead they discuss what to buy Will's son for his birthday that would appropriately counteract their anxious insecurities as the passers of the masculine torch ("a bag of hookers, an alligator," etc.). Strangely, or perhaps tellingly, the labor that these white-collar men do within the show's narratives is irrelevant, as if talking about jobs is verboten in a recession where the average viewer has either lost their job or has taken a pay cut or furlough. Where the true conflict lies is within themselves, shared between these three men, them against the world (and their children, wives, and other men). The rest of the episode consists of Kenny meeting his ex-wife's new African-American beau, Grant and challenging him to a game of one-on-one basketball (which he promptly loses, but only after Grant takes off his shirt, revealing an athletic muscularity directly the opposite of Kenny's overweight, short physique). It is worth noting that Grant is kind, sincere, can talk to women (he goes on about how "Pilates changed my life") and is fairly gorgeous—a seemingly model 'new man.'[11] Here we see an odd flip of the 'other,' so that Grant is everything the white dudes aren't (and can't be), and yet Grant is also cast as a bit of an object for the women. Theresa asks what Brenda is doing, implying that she's brought Grant to upset Kenny, even asking, "Well, what's his last name then?" Brenda replies, "Please, does he even need one?" After this, the three guys pile into the car under the guise of getting Will's son a 'real' birthday present (Grant bought him a shaving kit!), but they end up in front of the church where Henry's ex-girlfriend is getting married. Henry runs into the church with his acoustic guitar and plays "Brown Eyed Girl," while Kenny and Will watch, flabbergasted. Cut to the three of them running out of the church, the entire male wedding party in tow, promising violence, finishing at Will's house with a standoff, the dudes (and Grant) in the house, the angry wedding mob in front of the house. The dudes talk themselves up—"What an over-evolved generation of pantywaists we've become!"— and muster the courage to face the 10 angry men outside. And, of course, the women do nothing to stop it, fascinated by how 'out of character' their men are acting, presumably excited by the promise of violence in service of home and hearth. After a few threats, Grant suddenly charges and tackles at least three of the wedding party in a wild frenzy. The dudes stare in amazement. Cut to interior scene, the dudes eating birthday cake celebrating their win, even though Grant was the only one who fought and was subsequently arrested. Well, that gets rid of the black dude! The not-so-subtle racism here is palpable—Grant is the 'authentic, originary' black male body, the one who can play sports, fight, and, mirroring a national epidemic in the U.S., is incarcerated while the white middle-class men eat cake around the kitchen island. Of course, the men's fete is short-lived when Brenda tells Kenny to drive her to the police station to bail out Grant (easy bail for a black man who 'attacked' a group of white men, if only it were that easy), to which Kenny complies subserviently. The episode ends with Will giving his son a pocket-knife, as well as the violent videogame. Seconds later, we hear an off-screen wail, and then "Mom, I'm bleeding!"

In comparison to the other sitcoms in the new, male-centered group, *Man Up!* is the most confused about its purpose. Are they celebrating men now, or men then? Are they apologizing for the current soft state of masculinity, making fun of it, or offering solutions to fix it? I sense that, particularly since the show was canceled so quickly, the producers and writers weren't really sure either. The press, on the other hand, wasn't confused. Toby Lowry, writing for *Variety*, wrote, "How long can they play this joke? Isn't it really time to let go of stereotypes and clichés and maybe write a sitcom that has more to joke about than one thing over and over again?" And, from the same review:

> Remember "Traffic Light," which was on Fox, like, last season? It was only the most recent kinda-funny casualty in the male-panic genre, in which suburban trios of guys expose their inner Peter Pans, mostly by playing videogames and whining. In that regard think of ABC's "Man Up!"—paired with "Last Man Standing" in a thematically compatible if not particularly appealing block—as "The Hangover: Part TV," exploring the tired question of whether modern times have produced an over-evolved generation of girly men. Alas, it'll take more than sociology to pump up this stale sitcom.[12]

The moniker, "male-panic genre" is telling, as is Lowry's complaint regarding "whining," as it signifies that even within the genre *itself*, men aren't allowed to whine, or by extension, engage in stereotypical feminine behavior. And, the 'real' question, as it were, 'have modern times produced an over-evolved generation of girly men?' begs another, more complex question—what does 'over-evolved' mean? And what does this say about masculinity and essentialism? Clearly, 1) men are still presumed to be animals, and 2) they are capable of over-evolving to the point that they're in opposition to their true selves. Allegedly, women have been the cause of this over-evolution, so that men have been *forced* into the domestic, stripped of their muscles and basic instincts, not only against their will, but in opposition to a kind of natural, scientific and highly rationalized cultural (and biological) evolution. And, what to make of the line, "Alas, it'll take more than sociology to pump up this stale sitcom"? Is Lowry concerned about using sociological data to drive the creative process, or about writers who reflect current cultural trends and issues? The key here lies in the use of the term "pump up," a carefully chosen word that intimates the culture of body-building. So, Lowry didn't much like the show itself, but also the manner in which men are represented in the show. This, again, is at the core of the crisis of masculinity within the margins—the other guy is at-odds with his own at-odds-ness even though his anxieties and desires are still front and center on national television. He's still the center of attention, but now sees himself as struggling to get back to the center, both stalwart subject and victimized patsy.

In a more general review of the genre, Tim Goodwin (*The Hollywood Reporter*) writes:

> One of television comedy's most regrettable trends continues when ABC launches *Man Up!* on Oct. 18. You don't even have to be told the trend in question. You can see it in the show title. CBS has already relegated its weak-man comedy, *How to Be a Gentleman*, to Saturdays because of low ratings. NBC gave a full season order to *Up All Night*, which features Will Arnett as the stay-at-home dad trying to figure out his role (in the show's defense, the pilot was funny and it has a stellar cast with Christina Applegate and Maya Rudolph and Arnett's character isn't constantly questioning his manhood—but it's in the same zip code). To its credit, Fox doesn't have one of these shows. Perhaps to make up for that oversight, ABC has two. Tim Allen's *Last Man Standing* leads right into *Man Up!*, giving the country an hour of men worrying out loud that men have become Ken dolls (there's nothing down there) in the modern world.[13]

Goodwin seems a bit more critical of the form and content of these shows, even going so far as to point out the fact that it's the men themselves doing the 'worrying out loud,' while mentioning two women that feature in prominent roles. He also identifies their anxieties as based in their emasculation—as Ken dolls—partners to Barbies, anatomically neutered male dolls for girls, presumably to fill a girl's needs for heteronormative playthings, along with the dream house and pink Corvette.

Men at Work and The Big Other

If *Man Up!* is a marker of resistance within middle-class white men, robbed of their machoness and longing for methods to rekindle their penis power, *Men at Work*, created by mischief maker and everlasting-boy, Breckin Meyer (previously featured in teen and young adult raunchy comedies, and co-creator of boyhood dream-come-true TV show *Robot Chicken*, where action figures are staged in short, absurdist skits), is a return to the male sex comedies of the previous two decades. The series, now in its second season with a third on the way, centers on an other guy, the bearded and thoroughly average-looking Milo, who in the pilot episode, has just been dumped by his girlfriend. His first words upon hearing her declare her independence are revealing: "Lisa, baby, calm down, you're being hysterical, "to which she answers, "I don't love you anymore and I don't want to be in this relationship." Milo not only calls her "baby" (a pet name, but also a infantilization of her and her emotions), he also refers to her behavior as "hysterical," a word that has a bleak history stemming from the work of misguided and misogynistic male doctors, dating back thousands of years throughout Europe, and more famously during Victorian England, where a woman's 'hysterical' behavior was thought to be a product of her uterus (hence the term 'hysterectomy'), as well as in the early psychoanalytic theories of Freud, Janet and Breuer.[14] What follows is a series of jump-cuts between Milo in the break room of his workplace, surrounded by his three buddies (and co-workers) and Milo in a series of fantasy scenes where he acts out his misogynistic pipedreams in the face of Lisa abandoning him (he is, of course, stoned at the time—which functions as some kind of bland narrative excuse for his daydreams). These are interspersed with flashbacks detailing what actually happened, cued by his friends questioning the validity of his stories. The audience is left with a layered, post-postmodern pastiche of real and fantasy scenes, all of which are grounded in a masculine sphere of 'sharing,' yet one where fantasy is always met with a certain amount of blasé irony, as if growing up—truly growing up—would rob them of their inner, truthful imaginary.

His friends are the typical panoply of masculine other-guy figurations found in the 'mancom,' and all work for *Full Steam*, a fictional men's lifestyle magazine: Neal (a reporter), the geeky, bespectacled clueless buddy who is the only one in a committed relationship with a woman, Tyler (features writer), the pretty boy and metrosexual alpha male, and Gibbs (photographer), the ladies man and player, who, in an interesting change, is African-American. It's important, then, to note here that the other guy isn't necessarily always white, and not necessarily 'average'—the other guy is as much an attitude (and 'attitude' really) as he is a physique. These guys are all, needless to say, straight, in their 20s or early 30s, fairly attractive and written as good-hearted (when it counts). (The female characters are either non-existent or hollow, usually present as 'eye-candy.') The men all face the usual mélange of young male quandaries, which is to say most revolve around women. But, the other guy issues arise in interesting and complex ways in this sitcom. Neal pretends to be asleep to avoid having sex with his over-sexed and ravenous girlfriend, a woman who always seems to be home, calling from bed. When he mentions this, Milo scoffs, to which Neal must (of course) reply, "I'm not gay!" So, the requisite homophobia is present, but not always as a violent affirmation of straight sexuality. Instead the men affirm their heterosexuality in a variety of ways that always appear to be an *effort*, as if this too is a drag, along with work and relationships, and well, pretty much everything. Their (and the writers,' of course) efforts at misogyny feel forced, as if the material is a bit dated, and the actors know they are involved in a dying form—and, within the world of the show itself, they work for a dying industry, and at an increasingly desperate genre of men's magazine. (Whether this is a product of the overwhelming presence of digital media—particularly social media like Facebook and Twitter—and the performativity necessary for 'success' in this realm, or as a reflection of the culture itself suddenly becoming interested in them as a transitional, and often comic/tragic, masculinity, the other guys in this show clearly are meant as reflections of men in the world that have become soft because of the ubiquitous reliance on digital technologies.

While out at a bar, they term a woman with an extremely artificial tan, "whorange," mixing 'whore' and 'orange.' But, again, the delivery doesn't look or feel quite right. Signs of this have been seen for years, particularly in the performances of both Jon Cryer and Angus T. Jones in *Two and a Half Men*, half in response to Charlie Sheen's violent, disgusting and embarrassing behavior and half due to Chuck Lorre's equally tired and sexist executive production.[15] Additionally, Tyler, during a night out at a bar with the guys, ends up defending a male celebrity in what amounts to an act of real fraternity, yet which is still tainted by self-interest. The previous day, Tyler had tried and failed to get an interview out of said celebrity, so that when he sees him necking with a male at the bar, he quickly walks away to avoid embarrassing him (the celebrity is in the closet, evidently, which in itself is strange in relation to what happens next). The star sees him and bolts over to explain and in doing so, ends up bumping into a marked denizen of hip masculinity—the 'bro.' Now, the bro is an interesting invention of the 1990s and 2000s. They are almost always white and straight, and wear a very particular style: bejeweled shirts made famous by designer Ed Hardy, wallet chains, silver jewelry including earrings and rings, loose-fitting jeans (as opposed to the more hip tight fitting jeans popular more currently) and trimmed and primped hair.

In many ways, they are a strange byproduct of *Queer Eye for the Straight Guy* (a self-improvement show airing in the 2000s where a team of gay men take an average straight man and refashion him into a hipper, better groomed and more contemporary male) and *Jersey Shore* (an infamous reality show featuring a trashy cast of coiffed, manicured and dressed women and men from New Jersey who behave poorly and drink themselves silly). The Jersey Shore men in themselves are a conundrum—they work out relentlessly, shave every part of themselves, tan constantly, and refer to themselves as real, authentic, unapologetically (sexist) Italian men (although most of them are mixed Latino and Caucasian decent). But, at root, they care for their appearances at a level that rivals female TV and film actors and celebrities, so that this macho-ness always seems strangely at odds with their carefully maintained 'look.' So, bros are a more white-bread version of this man, probably finding some of their roots in white swing-dance and hot-rod culture, the cult of James Dean and films like 1996's *Swingers*.[16] Returning to *Men at Work*, the bro (unnamed in the show) threatens the star, and Tyler steps in. After Tyler stands up for the celebrity, he calls the bro out, even calling him 'Dane Cook,' after the guilt-macho stand-up comedian and actor (a pretty accurate example), and stating that he will close his eyes and let the bro punch him in the face if he doesn't have a particular kind of tattoo endemic to bros, the arm band, a tattoo that circles the bicep, meant to accentuate the muscularity of the male upper arm as well as signal a kind of modern primitive affiliation, as many of the tattoo motifs are taken from traditional, non-white cultures (Polynesian, in particular). So, while the bro may see himself as authentic in several dimensions, in this scene, by standing up for the gay celebrity (who wears a soft scarf piled around his neck, a signifier of a fairly new, more 'fay' and artistic masculinity), Tyler out-authenticizes him and the bro skulks away in distressed confusion. The reality here is that in an actual bar, the bro, surrounded by his bro buddies, would have punched Tyler immediately. However, what the writers and producers are saying here is something different, as Tyler, because of his 'heroics,' ends up getting the interview in the end. To Tyler, and to his friends, what matters is the chase and having the 'cajones' (a oft-used Spanish slang for testicles) to do what you need to do for results. Same old story, really, but here the other guy is marketed as the protector of 'the gays,' the straight guy with the heart of gold.

Conflict with an older male, usually a Baby Boomer or the equivalent, is of course part and parcel of this show, and features prominently in Episode 2 of Season 1, "Milo Full of Grace." The excellent JK Simmons plays Neal's potential father-in-law, who also happens to be owner and CEO of the magazine where the guys all work. He is rich, grouchy, and ruthlessly tough on Neal and the dudes, but particularly Neal, as he doesn't measure up to what his daughter deserves. Simmons' character, PJ, measures up the men while they lounge in the breakroom, frozen in place by his unannounced visit: "So, you're the guys that are supposed to know what's hip? [to Tyler] You look like a girl I dated in Switzerland. [to Milo] You look like a hobo. [to Neal] You're hopeless. [to Gibbs] And you, you're ok." So, here the aging patriarch knows that the line is drawn at race in 2012 (James Lesure, who plays Gibbs, is also the most famous of the actors who play the guys, so the writers might be playing nice here), while he still retains his disapproving bite. After Neal attempts to win favor with his future father-in-law, PJ admonishes him to make cuts at the magazine or his buddies will find themselves out of work. Neal then spends the remainder of the episode downsizing and economizing various aspects of the magazine and the office, and yet, his job title is 'reporter.' While this may be a bit of lazy storytelling, it's interesting in that the patriarch sends the meek Neal to do his dirty work, signaling the general distress that Boomer men feel in relation to younger men. There are countless examples, particularly in TV commercials, where older men bemoan the younger generation's lack, as fathers, as workers, as men in general. This trend is part of a more general and sweeping series of generational conflicts that have always been present, but it seems to have been ratcheted up by the four-year long recession beginning in 2008 (culminating in the Tea Party's overt racism and disgust with a younger, educated, black president, as well as with the youth vote responsible for his central campaign slogans, "Hope" and "Change"). So, in *Men at Work*, the young men who (hardly) work are the ones who have to clean up the mess, although nobody seems to want to take responsibility for the mess. Presumably, these are the particular corporate men who were supporters of men like Bill Clinton (who oversaw massive deregulation of financial markets) and/ or George W. Bush (who increased federal spending while overseeing one of the largest tax cuts in U.S. history). However, this portrayal of turmoil within the male identity between generations is, in many ways, a fiction, but a necessary one, ensuring that 'proving' as a means of articulating one's masculinity remains central to male social and political life. In short, other guys seem to be downright decent guys, but how can they win when the cards are so heavily stacked against them? They can't please their fathers, they are too much like their mothers, they don't work enough, their wives are better educated and their kids don't respect them. What is most remarkable about this self-assigned victimhood is that there are so many sitcoms—shows that are built around situations that are comic—that attempt to not only document these poor saps' situations, and that the shows actively engage in the construction of white, middle-class male victimhood. Clearly, this is a laughing matter, but it's more the laughter of the clown, despondent under the makeup, costumes and glare of the lights. An essential point needs to be clarified: masculine, prideful regression isn't just celebrated in the scripts, but in the media's form as well, particularly in the presence of a laugh track, more simplistic staging choices (rarely more than three sets are used), and the use of the two-camera set-up popularized by the first sitcoms of the 1950s.

In Slavoj Žižek's article, "Will You Laugh for Me, Please?" the author finds that canned laughter, or the laugh track, serves as a symptom of a larger cultural phenomenon, particularly since the laugh track blinds us to a paradox inherent to the genre and spectating in general. Žižek posits that, with the presence of a laugh track, the TV laughs in our place, so that our most intimate feelings become, "radically externalized."[17] While this process works for emotions, it also works at the level of belief. (He uses Santa Claus as an example, where parents believe it so their children believe it, and vice-versa,) These beliefs seem to work at a distance, so that the distance ensures that the "ultimate guarantor is always deferred, displaced, never present in the person." Thinking of Žižek's volumes of work, the Slovenian philosopher continually returns to the notion of deferral, the process of never getting what you want, a process built to ensure that one may escape/avoid the total psychic implosion that would inevitably follow. We aren't meant to get what we want, otherwise desire itself would be evacuated, our drives would end, and representation itself would grind to a halt. A central tension when it comes to consuming sitcoms with laugh tracks, and in essence, nearly all digital representation, lies between interactivity and interpassivity. Žižek finds that because it is so often assumed that when dealing with a screen, we must *interact*—co-write the text, manipulate the avatar, participate in nascent democracy—that we have been deprived of the act of *passively* watching the box. He finds this inner world, whether through laughter or sadness (or boredom), is robbed from us through interactivity, but also through the laugh track—would you laugh for me, please (I'm too tired)? Like a man laughing furiously after a tasteless joke, the laugh track isn't an anonymous studio audience, it's the narrator himself, and s/he is doing the laughing (much like the dopey plink-plunk music in romcoms that is present, it seems, only to *remind* us that something dopey is happening, even while we watch it unfold). Moving to his brand of distinct and evocative

Hegelian/Lacanian analysis, Žižek theorizes that this ensures, "the inscription of his act into the Big Other," or the larger symbolic order. But, this is a problem; if we allow, "an imaginary dialogue between ourselves and the Big Other to remain incomplete, we commit ourselves to symbolic oblivion." Or, if we don't do the laughing, or, more to the point, if someone does the laughing for us, we are failing to be the kind of ontological subject Žižek finds most fruitful, one who is active in the construction of discourse, while they are aware of their complicit 'subjectedness.' Continuing, Žižek connects this scenario to labor, finding that the laugh track and its fellow travelers operate as a kind of stand-in for other activities that the laboring subject should be engaged in as a means of *respite* from labor, i.e., leisure, play, etc. "The real threat of the new media is they deprive us of our passivity, or our authentic passive experience, and thus prepare us for mindless frenetic activity—for endless work."

So, then what's going on when we watch *Men at Work*, a show with a laugh track featuring actors with laboring bodies, about men who don't really work, who constantly chase women and leisure? Is there a difference in the way that we watch shows like *Last Man Standing* and *Men at Work*, because they have laugh tracks? Is there a difference in the meaning-making, particularly for male viewers? Perhaps in the watching, we the audience take these men and their message—the meanings that they make (keeping in mind Žižek's formulation)—as proof-positive that men at work are in fact the unifying concept in contemporary masculinity, to the extent that a laugh track is necessary so that the men who watch can defer any passivity, including interpassivity. Is this yet another way that masculinity avoids any meaningful self-reflection, and also a way that men can feel that they are a) in on the joke (which is themselves), and b) laboring machines who never need leisure or passive activities? How then do these men navigate the Big Other, the symbolic order, if their bodies, their work, their *identities* are buttressed by media that continually, even at the structural level, require them to allay the passive, the reflective, the self-critical? In this sense, TV is functioning, in a highly efficacious way, as an, to dredge up Althusser, Ideological State Apparatus, particularly in the way that it both interpolates the viewer and controls the means of interpellation (in this case the nominal familiarity and normativity of the laugh track). And, what do we make of sitcoms that *don't* have a laugh track? Neither *Perfect Couples* nor *Man Up!* uses laugh tracks, instead following the single camera format, pursing their subjects into the space of the sets and realistic-looking locations. Obviously with the use of close-ups and a moving camera, as opposed to the set-camera arc of a live studio (which in many ways, still replicates the Realist theatre stage invented in the 1880s, with its 'radical' yet bourgeois trappings and domestic focus), we are thrust closer to the emotional states of the characters and are more involved in the reveals, surprises and internal states of these men. In single-camera set-ups, we watch their bodies in a more complete rhetorical fashion—we can see their 'flow' as actors and as characters—and the camera is more responsible for directing our eyes toward what the director or producers (or showrunner) want us to see. But this is fairly obvious.

And so I also would like to place Žižek's schema in proximity to masculinity itself, most distinctly the way other guys seem to lead their lives as if a laugh track is omni-present, and use this, by extension, to perform a vaguely apolitical, and yet presumed left-of-center personal politics. The rallying cry of this positionality is, of course, "Am I right?" This phrase, like the laugh of the tasteless joke-teller, is less a question than a simultaneous assertion of cloaked authority and an avoidance of the Big Other, by simple ontological mimesis of their own subjective and masculine (white) 'rightness.' In the end, "Am I right?" is really "I'm not gay," the ubiquitous denial of and abhorrence with male same-sex penetration (and the other attendant stereotypes, anxieties and hidden desires straight men associate with it). But, also, hidden in "Am I right?" is the admonition that passivity is the true man-killer, passivity akin to Žižek's schema. If we as viewers, and men as men, are robbed of their subjective passive inner experience of actually doing the laughing, a form of being male, then the laugh track crutch is essentially a stand-in for a kind of ideological hail requiring men to 'work' constantly at being men. Or, put another way, it is the process of never allowing themselves to operate outside of the closed circuit of proving. "I'm not gay" then serves as a marker of anxiety, reaction, conservatism, and distance, but also as a new means for other guys to negotiate the discrepancies of the new labor markets and their dwindling preeminence in these markets. During the recession in the U.S., numerous media sources constantly reported on the 'rise of women in the workplace' but in a tone different than the past 30 years of women's progress in labor, education and the social sphere. Women were now *better*-educated and returning to work *more quickly* than men, even with the attendant social 'crises' that haunt the women's movement and feminism (motherhood, domestic duties, workplace harassment, the glass ceiling, etc.). Men remained out of work longer and tended to 'give up' looking for work more quickly. This then was, of course, followed by a cultural diagnosis: men were suffering from 'low T' (low testosterone levels); they needed Cialis and Viagra to 'get it up;'

they had become emasculated by staying home and taking care of the kids. A cover of a *Newsweek* magazine from 2011 features a white, middle-aged man in a suit, lying on a beach, face down, under the headline, "The Beached White Male." Clearly, things were getting sketchy for these men. So, in many ways, the above sitcoms are a cultural psychoanalytic couch for all these poor guys and their worried families, but also for men in their 20s and early 30s who saw their fathers out of work, as well as their work possibilities all but dry up in the mid 2000s. The family castle was suddenly underwater, pensions disappeared and jobs were downsized or outsourced. So, were there any signs of hope? Any texts that played against the grain?

Phil Dunphy: Realtor, Dad, Magician

One notices immediately that *Modern Family* sets itself apart from the standard sitcom structure (neither with a live studio audience like *Men at Work* nor the standard single-camera setup of *Perfect Couples*) by using the mockumentary format, announcing its own precariousness as a piece of representational, network entertainment associated with the sitcom genre. All of the characters from each of the three central families on *Modern Family* are presented on camera in confessionals (usually the purview of reality shows) where they comment on each other's behavior, but also speak directly to the viewer and reveal a kind of 'truth' about each situation. This, of course has been used over the course of the last decade in shows such as *The Office* (both the U.K. and U.S. versions) and *Parks and Recreation*. Yet what sets *Modern Family* apart is that the confessional moments serve a structural and thematic purpose within the world of the show; they constantly work to draw the characters toward one another in order to highlight (if not literally celebrate) difference, while simultaneously emphasizing togetherness and familial continuity by frequently featuring several characters *together* in these confessionals. And, indeed, difference lies at the heart of the show, particularly in the drawing-room hijinks and eccentricities that each character experiences in relation to other characters and other families. While middle-class whiteness is core to the show, sexuality and gender difference feature quite prominently, particularly by way of a fairly functional gay male couple, Cameron and Mitchell, and their adoptive Vietnamese daughter, Lily. The other couples live in more stereotypical sitcom territory: the patriarch, Jay Pritchett, his voluptuous and passionate younger Colombian wife, Gloria, and their neurotic and old-soul son, Manny (from her previous marriage), along with a very young baby, Joe (from their current marriage). We also have the central family, led by Claire (Jay's daughter) and aided by eccentric other guy Phil Dunphy, and their kids, wild-child Haley (currently home from dropping out of college), middle child and prodigy Alex, and Luke, clueless and carefree, Phil's other guy acolyte. What stands out in this show, other than the fairly consistently funny dialogue and physical humor and critical and audience success, is how it *resembles* and *plays at* and *with* representations of various modern families. This is, of course, a mixed bag. While we have a positive and generally well-received gay couple who work well together as partners and as parents, there are still clear examples of sexism and troublesome gender stereotypes. For the first four seasons, none of the women have careers, and they are often forced into hiding their real talents in order to assuage the men. In episode 502, "First Days," Claire timidly shows up for her first day of work—at her father's business. Jay: "Sweetheart, you look terrific!" Claire: "Are you sure? Because I have another blouse in here [motioning to her briefcase]. It's the only thing in here. That and a pair of glasses in case I need to read something or look smart." So, Claire's initiative in re-joining the workforce (she quit her job when she became pregnant with Phil and her first child) is undercut by, a) her father's primary acknowledgment of her looks, b) her equal acknowledgment of her looks as primary, and c) her tone of defeat, which she states earlier in the episode, over going to work for her father instead of in a career free from nepotism. This is the tricky world of gender relations on *Modern Family*, a bit like sexuality on *Will & Grace*, where the progressive flourishes are often undercut by the more conservative structures and thematics so foundational in the American sitcom.

To continue, Claire's older daughter, Haley, uses her sexuality to get what she wants, and plays dumb when it serves her. Alex, the middle child, is brilliant, but she is also unable to connect with boys and seems more interested in taking down Haley, or at least what she represents for women. And yet, she's shown often as looking up to her. Gloria, Jay's wife, is the standard 'cougar' (a term circa mid-2000s for attractive, older women who are often labeled as predatory in their sexuality), hyper-emotional and often ditzy, and yet she is clearly an able schemer (but would never let Jay see this). The actress, Sofia Vergara, has been readily criticized for reinforcing Hispanic and Latina stereotypes; she is passionate, voluptuous and 'spicy.' Jay, on the other hand, takes the mantle of the *de facto* stud for bedding such a woman, although he is also rich. And, between Mitchell and Cameron (the gay couple),

Mitchell is a lawyer and Cameron is the stay-at-home parent. However, Cameron is sometimes the bottom—he is overweight, prone to hyperbolic emotional outbursts, and has a background in clowning, music and performance, but also figures as the top when he regularly rescues Mitchell from situations and problems (while also having been raised on a ranch). Mitchell is the intellectual, much shorter and slimmer than Cameron, and so can be assumed to be the bottom, except when it comes to sensible work and domestic choices. In this sense, their relationship avoids the simple duality of clear top/bottom, perhaps reflecting the reality of most gay male relationships.

In the midst of this one-step-forward, two-steps-back political/social representational dance, is Phil, the figurehead of the Dunphy clan, clueless, sweet and often engaged in one form of boyhood regression or similar familial scheme or prank. He is essentially the other guy who doesn't know he's the other guy, a modern man who cries and tries, but never really understands what's at stake in his particular form of masculinity. His work, as a realtor, is often satirized because of its innate dodginess and outsize ambition, but again, Phil doesn't seem to 'get' this, as he's often outmaneuvered by other competing realtors without ever losing his moxie. Add to this that the show premiered in 2009, at the low point of the housing crash, and it seems fairly likely that the producers and writers placed him in this line of work not for its disgust-potential, but as a symbol of American naïve economic over-prognostication and bountiful optimistic overreach. Phil believes he's selling the American dream. But he isn't very good at it, choosing instead to focus most of his time on keeping his house in order, which, if he had his choice, would probably look like a bouncy-house with magicians, toys and odd science experiments around every corner. Throughout the series, his masculinity is often the butt of the joke for the other men in the family, including his father-in-law, Jay, and his biological father, played by the terminal jokester, Fred Willard, star of the Christopher Guest mockumentaries *Waiting for Guffman, Best in Show* and *A Mighty Wind.* (In many ways, his presence on the show serves as a kind of ode to Guest's pioneering work in this genre.) However, the show itself seems more intent on a kind of pedagogical masculinity through all of its characters, both male and female, so that masculinity and its attendant performances are configured as processes of trial and error, consisting of a rather optimistic, open-ended set of opportunities (and funny situations) for masculine progression and evolution.

In the episode "The Last Walt," four central conflicts occur. First, the Dunphy's next-door neighbor, Walt (a retired single man who is never shown) dies suddenly and Claire becomes concerned with their son Luke's seemingly apathetic attitude toward his death, as the two were friends during past years. Second, Cameron's father, Merl (a tough-guy, can-do cowboy) visits and engages in a long-standing feud with Mitchell's father, Jay. Third, Phil becomes obsessed with creating the perfect bonding moment for him and his daughter, Alex. And fourth, Manny (Jay and Gloria's 13-year-old son) is cajoled by Haley into being the 'adult' chaperone for a teenage pool party at Jay and Gloria's spacious and meticulous modern home. In all of these plot lines, masculinity and male roles are argued about, displaced, questioned and finally solidified in favor of clear gender divides and well-maintained male roles. Perhaps the most telling of the conflicts lies between Merl and Jay, as they are both concerned that each of them treats the other's son like the 'woman' in the relationship. Jay growls at Merl when he gives the Mitchell and Cameron watches and Mitchell receives the smaller, more 'feminine' watch. This leads to a comedic inversion typical of the show in that Mitchell and Cameron, after discussing that their two fathers seem to be getting on well, begin to subtly snipe at each other, with both claiming that their father is the more butch of the two. This results in several things. Jay and Merl, after putting together Mitchell and Cameron's new box spring for their bed (thus treating them both like the 'wife,' as all real men should surely know how to build things), sit on the bed together (in itself, a nice physical bit) and realize what they are both doing. Merl reluctantly says, "It makes me feel a tiny bit better to think that the person he's spending his life with is a tiny bit of a woman," signaling his conditional support of their partnership, but also his (and, by proxy, his generation's) inability to think beyond traditional gender roles. "I guess we've got no choice," he continues. Jay then says, exhaustedly, "We've got two sons and they're both gay for each other." This further amplifies the two men's inability to not only think beyond stereotypes, but also creates humor out of their inability to *speak* beyond 'norms' ("they're gay for each other"). Yet, Mitchell and Cameron's duel remains unresolved, which is odd for the show, as during this season, the show began to spend the last minutes of each episode in an orgasm of resolution, complete with sappy music and narration about how family is both tough and wonderful, a distinct departure from previous seasons' relative non-melodramatic closings. Revisiting Mitch and Cam's conundrum, their 'contest' (essentially, whose dad has a bigger dick) is left out in the open, signaling possibly their inability as gay men to understand the pressures of 'real' manhood, effectively placing them (like the fathers did) in the roles of dual wives, stuck in an endless domestic battle and cat-fight. It's fairly rare for U.S. sitcoms to feature a not-quite-happy ending with little closure; the final episode of *Seinfeld* taught studios not to mess with the formula. However, when it comes to straight masculinity, we get a happy ending in the form of Phil and Alex, finally sharing their bonding moment together.

In the scene, Phil recounts a story of an astronaut who scrawled his daughter's initials on the moon's surface and how he and other fathers can never live up to that kind of pressure. Alex demurely agrees. Yet, as they finish their meal at the Moonlight Café and walk outside, Phil impulsively scrawls her initials on the moon encircling the café's glowing sign, and they drive away, both visibly re-bonded and happy. And so this semiotic act, writing a name on a sign that already speaks for itself, marking it for others to see, this is what's available to the other guy, the casual defacing of property, as much a teenage act of rebellion as something done by lovers in the bark of a tree. Bonding with his daughter, it turns out, is as much an act of traditional romanticism as it is a return to boyhood and its attendant rule-breaking. This act of proving, mired in the sacred strangeness of father/daughter relationships (complicated constantly by the oversexualization of young women in the media and literalized in the show by the ever-present sexuality of Haley) positions Phil as still weakly attracted to the pissing-territorialism of the young guy with something to prove. And yet he is also distinctly marked as lesser by other men who feature on the show, because of things like this sweet-natured quest to bond with his daughter, surely a productive form of proving in service of his relationship with one of his daughters. These are the kind of choices he is ridiculed for in his continued hapless and deluded naiveté throughout the show. Being an astronaut certainly isn't in the stars for poor Phil, but it's not because of the women in the show. Or anyone else. Phil remains teathered to the average by his other guyness, a situation he would probably just shrug off before he showed his next magic trick.

Notes

1. From the ESQ website: "…a lifestyle and entertainment network featuring programming that speaks to classic and contemporary passions and interests, from fashion and style to food and drink, travel and women and relationships." In other venues, the channel is described as aimed at the "metrosexual" market. It debuted in September of 2013. http://tv.esquire.com/

2. Raymond Williams, *Marxism and Literature*, 1977.

3. See Julie D'Acci's, "Women Characters and 'Real World' Femininity," (pp. 100–143), as well as "The Front Row Is Reserved for Scotch Drinkers," (pp. 451–469), both in *Television, The Critical View*, Ed. Horace Newcomb. Oxford: Oxford U. Press, 2000, for two

excellent, gender-focused readings of not only TV texts, but the spaces that became articulated by the TV as device.

4. Michael Kimmel, *Manhood in America: A Cultural History*. New York: The Free Press, 1996.
5. Charlotte Brunsdon, "What Is the 'Television' of Television Studies?" in *Television: The Critical View*, pp. 609–610 (609–628).
6. Rebecca Feasey, *Masculinity and Popular Television*. Edinburgh: Edinburgh U. Press, 1998, p. 20.
7. Feasy, 31.
8. And, as with *Home Improvement*, *Last Man Standing* garners approximately 8–9 million viewers per show, on par with other male-centered, blockbuster sitcoms like *Seinfeld, 2 ½ Men* and *Everybody Loves Raymond*.
9. Benjamin, Walter. "Unpacking my Library," *Illuminations*, Harry Zohn, trans, Fontana, London, 1973, 63.
10. Ibid., 62.
11. I learned (much to my chagrin), while writing this book, that a term exists for this specific type of awesome, jealousy-inducing black guy—he's a 'Derek.'
12. Review: *Man Up!*, Toby Lowry, *Variety*, posted Oct. 16, 2011. Retrieved June 10, 2013.
13. *Man Up!*: TV review, Tim Goodman, *Hollywood Reporter*, Posted Oct. 11, 2011. Retrieved June 8, 2013.
14. See Tanya Wexler's light-hearted but fascinating film *Hysteria* (2011) for an interesting narrativization of early gynecology and the invention and application of the first 'personal massage devices,' or, vibrators, or Almodóvar's *Women on the Verge of a Nervous Breakdown*.
15. In 2012, Jones went so far as to call himself a "paid hypocrite," as he found the show to be in conflict with his religious views. So, here I don't mean to mark him as a feminist, but as a performer at odds with his material. Perhaps as an acknowledgment of changes in audience expectation and larger cultural shifts since the show's inception in 2003, the producers will be adding a female character to replace Jones. See Cowell, Maria (November 27, 2012). How 'Two and a Half Men' Star Became a 'Paid Hypocrite.' *Christianity Today*.
16. In many ways, two of the films stars qualify as early other guys, Jon Favreau and Rod Livingston, and yet Vince Vaughn (who's first major role was in *Swingers*) remains the most visible, playing smooth-talking but emotionally vulnerable characters in countless films. What should be clear here is that many male actors who qualify as other guys in their characterizations also try to cultivate that other guyness as real men.
17. Slavoj Žižek, "Will You Laugh for Me, Please," *InTheseTimes.com*, July 18, 2003, retrived August 29, 2012.

· 4 ·

SOMEWHERE IN THERE THERE'S A MAN IN THERE

"Within the soul of even the most die-hard constructionist lurks a doubt. It is
called the body."

—Anne Fausto-Sterling,
From "How to Build a Man"

"My mantra? Always go the extra mile…to treat my low T."

—TV ad for Axiron, a testosterone replacement drug

In a series of recent print advertisements, the men's fragrance company Old
Spice has enunciated a common dichotomy at the heart of the contemporary
man—the inner schmuck and the outer star.

In the ads, a quarter of the male is cut away (his torso and head), as if
he's a 3D topographical map, to reveal a Ramboesque mercenary soldier,
and in the second a heavy-metal rock star. The first external guy stands in a
wood-paneled library, festooned with geek glasses, a casual t-shirt and chi-
nos. The second is a meek-looking, overweight 'mama's boy' in an elevator,
wrapped up in a knitted and patterned sweater, scarf and beanie, presumably
heading outside to weather the cold in comfy wimpiness.[1] The tag line at
the bottom of the advertisement, "Smell Better Than Yourself," communicates a key truth for the other guy—the real you will never stack up, so

use our product (albeit ironically) and maybe you will. But the ads also say something else, through that ironic pose; men have grown comfortable with the notion that they have to perform something that they intrinsically are 'not,' nor will ever be, and here, it's access to the mindset, the scenario—life as a videogame avatar—that's the draw. Also at play here is the pull of essentialist authenticity versus postmodern performativity, except here, in these ads, the authentic interior of the subject is the performance, while the undesirable external is a series of eliding signifiers without a referent. So, Old Spice (a brand that has embraced the ironic hipsterism of the 2000s), the smell of it and what pleasures it will bring you, serves as emblematic of the tension within the other guy. A similar print ad from Gillette Fresh and Clean Body Wash features a picture of a man exiting the shower, naked and completely 'manscaped' (where nearly all of the hair on a man's body is removed—particularly the chest, back and stomach, and presumably the genitals), with an inset of him on the phone at the office wearing a neatly pressed tie and shirt. Again, the subtext here is that if the 'underneath' man—the hidden but essential traits—is manicured and has that 'just-out-of-the-shower' feeling, the external man remains firmly tethered to what remains indispensable. And, to boot, a co-worker (ostensibly, a subordinate) in a hardhat stands in the background of the labor-site inset. Real men, men who run construction sites, use body wash—in fact, the guys that do clearly make it into management!

Similarly, an Art of Shaving ad (a men's 'handsomeness' care line) admonishes men to, "Repeat after us: I will not shave 'economy' when 'first class' is available.' Welcome to the brotherhood of shaving," solidifying the link between masculinity, a clean shave, class and access to *the* network of men who are successful and, more significantly, at the edge of a trend that recognizes men's beauty products as an extension of power, instead of vanity, femininity or 'gayness.' Finally, an ad for Nivea for Men Q10 Revitalizing Double Action Shave Gel and Balm featuring a clean-cut 30-something white guy in a suit and tie, mixed race friends chatting in the background on a dazzling-lights city street, asks, "Would a member of the Rat Pack have set foot on the Las Vegas strip looking anything less than perfectly tailored, clean shaven and impeccably groomed? Or dared to hit the baccarat tables with two days' worth of beard stubble?" Now, this ad is telling (and clever) on several levels. First, by referencing the Rat Pack and Las Vegas, Nivea is thoroughly applying the nostalgia, but a nostalgia that has waxed and waned in various historical forms and moments (from the *Swingers*-induced swing dance craze of the mid '90s, the return of the martini and cigar in the late '90s, or to the craft beer and boutique spirits boom of the mid-2000s), a wistfulness that consistently sets itself *in opposition* to whatever current, contemporaneous men's counterculture that advocates for a more hippie-centric outlook or bohemian lifestyle (for instance, at the time of this writing, this ad would not be aimed at men living in Brooklyn, Silver Lake [L.A.], or the Haight-Ashbury). But, what it also does is tell the dude that there are some things you just have to clean up for, like Las Vegas, and by doing this, it again tightens the cord around the messy excesses of the inner male by grooming the outer male, and, strangely enough here, vice versa. So, the male body becomes an evolving project—a far cry from the stereotypical (and too often celebrated) rigidity, solidity and Spartan resistance to contingency that is expected of and policed in everyday men. It looks (and smells) like men are recognizing not only their interior and exterior, but how they work together to produce an evolving project, even if it is through visibility projects and competing beauty standards.

In a much more general sense, new products and marketing strategies have begun to acknowledge the changing role of men in relation to the domestic sphere, pegging them not only as shoppers, but as equally responsible for child-rearing, cooking and other household duties. In a survey conducted by Midian Marketing LLC, a Chicago-based marketing firm focused on the meat industry, 900 men, ages 18–64, were asked about their grocery shopping and food preparation habits; 47% were identified as "manfluencers," or men who were responsible for at least half of the shopping and cooking in their households.[2] Thus, a variety of products have been reshaped or repackaged to appeal to male consumers who are drawn to signifiers and aesthetics such as darker colors, more substantial and bulky fonts, and words like "Ultimate" (like the new Ultimate Hamburger Helper) and "Pro" (from the new ProYo Frozen Yogurt). This shift has been going on for years in the alcohol industry, with hard ciders showing the greatest shift, away from the sweet, bubbly beverages typically assumed to be the purview of women (such as Wyder's or Woodchuck brands, with their colorful, friendly labeling), to the more 'manly' Pete's Hard Lemonade (again, featuring a black label with an industrial stamped font), the canned (not bottled) Smith and Forge Cider, with a higher alcohol content and the slogan "Made Strong" on the label, and the Ace brand ciders, featuring playing cards on the label. Stephen Colbert, on his show *The Colbert Report* (a 'fake news' program that airs weeknights on the Comedy Central channel) recently poked fun at "manfluencers" in his

"Thought for Food" segment, where he assumed his usual chauvinist, reactionary right-wing character, the antithesis of Jon Stewart's actual, liberal, persnickety self on *The Daily Show* (which airs before *The Colbert Report*). Referring to the new product, Powerful Yogurt (with a bull's head and horns on the label), Colbert stated, "This yogurt is extra manly because evidently it's made from bull's milk. Very difficult to acquire. But the bull will thank you." That's food for (male) thought.

Throughout this chapter, I look at a variety of mediatized objects in an effort to get to the heart of the other guy's body and its proclivities, but also to understand how masculinity itself responds to its own perceived vulnerabilities and crises, how it is represented, bought and sold in popular media, with an eye toward the body's contradictions and excesses.

Men's Bodies, Men's Hearts

In his searching and expansive book, *Manhood in America*, Michael Kimmel traces a history of men in the U.S., not just as men, but as men who have shaped the country and been shaped by it, but with the implicit understanding that *masculinity* itself undergoes shifts and upheavals, regularly and often spectacularly. In his chapter "Wimps, Whiners and Weekend Warriors: The Contemporary Crisis of Masculinity and Beyond," Kimmel identifies tactics and trends which have been promulgated by men while also being presumably forced upon them from a host of external forces. Kimmel finds that, "…the manhood regained under Presidents Regan and Bush was the compulsive masculinity of the schoolyard bully, defeating weaker foes such as Grenada and Panama, a defensive and restive manhood, of men who needed to demonstrate their masculinity at every opportunity."[3] In this sense, masculinity is both a reaction to the heightened economic and political power of the nation-state, as well as an extension of that power into the community, labor and personal spheres. And yet, Kimmel adds that in many ways American men were more confused than ever during the 1980s, whether from the rise of feminism, the fallout from Vietnam and Watergate, as well as the rise of notions like the 'new Age man,' a guy who is sensitive, emotive and receptive to women's perceived indecipherability. At the same time, many men and, "Some women rejected the wimp as well. Wimps weren't invested in sharing power or equality, some women complained; they simply wanted to abdicate breadwinning responsibility."[4] This situation is humorously depicted in the 1983 film, *Mr. Mom*, where Michael Keaton plays one of these 'new men' who, after being fired from his job, offers to take over the household responsibilities so that his wife can climb the corporate ladder, with shades of the other guy surfacing in his relationship to his kids and wife. Throughout the film, he is at constantly odds with his new domestic role, gains weight, grows a beard and gets depressed, but manages to whip the house into shape and get his former job back, his wife feeling guilty over not spending enough time with the kids. Decades later, we as a culture are still struggling with the place of men in the domestic, but it seems clear that economics and cultural backlash are still the key driving factors in the shaping of men's lives and progress toward more equitable relationships with their partners and families.

Reacting to the perceived emasculating push of the 'feminazis,' men in the '80s and '90s engaged in one of many reactions, both physical and emotional, that would become a structural-historical normative process, continuing up to the present. This wave-form is comprised of cultural or economic shifts that represent how normative/non-normative male behavior undergoes peaks and valleys (an economic downturn, a new film genre, a health or psychological study/breakthrough, a presidential administration, etc.), so that a certain percentage—let's call them 'early adopters'—embrace the new behaviors, ideas, and sensibilities, and then how the more recalcitrant men react and reject these new waves. This process, of course, corresponds in several ways to Raymond Williams' concepts of the interplay of *dominant, residual,* and *emergent* forms and modes, and his focus on a more localized sense of cultural process and production, a move away from the more epochal notions of historical change of Hegel or Lukacs.[5] Kimmel identifies one of these reactions personified in the "angry white males":

> They say they are sick and tired of being oppressed by women and dominated by impersonal bureaucracies—and they're not going to take it anymore! They experience feminism as an 'emasculating force, for it exaggerates that familiar sense of unmanly guilt,' and today's man is fed up with the efforts to make him feel guilty. It's men who are the victims, they say. Politically, this resentment and anger has fueled a new gender gap, the preponderance of middle-class, middle-aged, straight white males who are listing constantly to the right. Raised to feel "entitled" themselves, they resent any entitlement program that gives anything to anyone else.[6]

What is remarkable about this passage is that Kimmel was writing in the mid-1990s, and here we are in the U.S. at the time of this writing witnessing a near identical reactionary melee over the Affordable Care Act, more commonly known as Obamacare. Certainly much of the resentment and anger over 'entitlement reform' has been fueled by the bully tactics of the Tea Party, the Fox News right-wing message machine, and the nation-wide frustration over the Wall Street corruption-driven recession, but the reaction can also be understood as one in a series of gender upheavals, this one aimed in particular at Obama's distinct masculine performance and other masculine formations that remain abhorrent to more traditional, 'patriotic,' recognizable and hegemonic masculinities, often in the form of burly, built and boisterous white male bodies. This is made plain in a number of ways: Putin's infamous shirtless, macho, barrel-chested photographs, contrasted with Obama's slender, 'intellectual' physique, one made for basketball instead of wrestling bears, or the widely distributed photos of President Obama body surfing during a family vacation in Hawaii, a distinctive sport that requires finesse and knowledge of waves and requires a physicality the polar opposite of an American football player.

Kimmel continues by citing President Clinton as the first 'new man' in the presidency, a policy wonk who smoked weed while at Oxford, with a 'ball-buster' of a wife, Hilary Rodham Clinton. At odds with this new man in the White House, the 1990s were peppered with men's movements that saw a return to the body as site of masculine power, from the Promise Keepers to extreme sports. Yet, this body-centered, excessive masculinity wasn't available or all that interesting to a wide array of men, and so we see the rise of 'escapism' for men, from videogames to man caves, the return of all male boxing gyms to Fantasy Football leagues. As Kimmel writes, "So where can me go to feel like men? This is one of the questions fueling the anger of the men's rights groups, who seek to prop up traditional definitions of masculinity in the ways that besieged men have always done: by clearing everyone else off the playing field."[7] A quintessential mode of escape, as opposed to athletic competition, has been (and remains) working out. During the '90s a rash of home-exercise equipment flooded the market, systems like Bowflex, which promise "Shorter Workouts. Better results." Coupled with male-focused health magazines like *Men's Health* and *Men's Fitness* and male-centered lifestyle magazines such as *Details*, the new health program promised to remake the man from head to toe, through workout regimes, dieting tips, fashion advice and relationship and dating columns. Of course, in *Details*, a sexy female (usually a film star, model or athlete) adorns the cover, complete with a soft-core picture piece, a more 'refined' version of the *Playboy* centerfold. Men were allowed, even encouraged to scope out the female body, but the new man preferred to couch his desires in the cloak of respectability. After all, the new man wasn't a sexist. But he still wanted to get laid. And look good doing it.

Yet there was also a contradictory tone throughout much of masculine popular discourse throughout the 1990s (particularly in regards to the body) that tainted the 'advances' men were making in their relationships with women and other men. While film and TV during the '80s and '90s continued to showcase hulking men with muscles (Schwarzenegger, Stallone, Gibson, etc.) disposing of bad guys with guns and fists, a deeper psychological battle was afoot—one that led back to their childhood psychological development and current symptomology. Again, Kimmel states, "Like their turn-of-the-century forbears, contemporary masculinists, argue that men today are listless, lifeless, enervated, feminized. Psychologically, they claim that this is because men have not adequately separated from their mothers."[8] However, the criticism leveled at the contemporary absent father (quite different from the noble absence of the WWII soldier) was largely based on rising expectations for fathers in general, and how these young men might underdevelop in the face of the absence of *their* fathers (who are working jobs with endless hours), and how this will effect their ability to grow up and 'man up.' This inability to 'man up' became a root cause for the assumed 'failures' of the generations of males following the first Gulf War, male bodies either marked as 'making the cut' or 'falling short.' This is where working out and bulking up comes in. These men (even if they had no athletic talent) could sculpt and maintain their bodies so they were ready for action, even if the dreamed-of bar-fight never materialized, or they had no intention of joining the military, police or emergency services. Simply watching primetime TV for a couple of hours can reveal just how homogenized and predictable these male bodies have become, with each male actor expected to have 'six-pack abs,' large 'pecs,' rippling biceps and an acceptable shade of tan and waxy-smooth skin. It is also during the 1990s that we see Viagra™ take root in the popular consciousness, as well as pharmaceuticals for 'low T,' yet another invented syndrome/disorder that plagued men after 30, as well as a rise in plastic surgery for men, particularly in hard-to-build areas of the male bodies (pectorals, calves, butts). And so, returning to the body map I introduced in Chapter 1, each of these spaces on the body correspond to particular male fads and the film and TV stars that promote them on infomercials and advertisements, or by simply showing them off on Thursday's episode.

Alongside this battle-ready workout mystique and culture sit the culture of videogames, particularly First Person Shooters like *Goldeneye*, *Doom* and the *Call of Duty* franchise where the player unconsciously identifies with the unseen avatar on screen, eyes sutured to the screen, witnessing only the end of the gun barrel and the bursts of fire accompanying each press of a controller button. So, during the 1990s and the 2000s, these workout regimens, coupled with prescribed testosterone, muscle-building additives and violent videogames solidified right alongside major socially and culturally progressive shifts such as the increased public discourse about rape and male violence (toward women as well as men) throughout the popular media (and in particular, on college campuses). But, the question was, and is, were men, at least on the surface, 'playing along' with changing cultural norms? Of course, in response to the depth and breadth of conversation around the utter unacceptability of rape and violence toward women, men withdrew (and escaped) by focusing on the two of the three areas of what Michael Kaufman has identified in the "Triad of Men's Violence," violence toward other men and violence toward themselves.[9] These three forms of violence are mutually imbricated and constative; the three corners of the triad reinforce one another. The first corner—violence against women—cannot be confronted successfully without simultaneously challenging the other two corners of the triad. And all of this requires a dismantling of the social feeding ground of violence: patriarchal, heterosexist, authoritarian, classist societies.

Considering this complex locus of factors, I argue that this over-focus on the building of the body, while couching it amongst the competing lifestyle categories of health, fashion, music, dating, etc., and with the rise of violent interactive media (as well as with the increased exposure and honest conversations about violence against women, while buttressed against the softer sexism of popular magazines like *GQ*, *Details* and *Esquire*) created a new-new man, what was commonly referred to as the metrosexual throughout the 2000s, a product of a rejection of the Alpha male, the Beta, and the outlier, or Omega male. Out of this set of social and body indexes, the other guy appears, an amalgamation of different male power positions and hierarchies, and the myriad body expectations and rules imposed on all men. Add to this the rise of the dotcom companies, Silicon Valley, digital social networks, massive online multiplayer videogames, and the bohemian bourgeoisie born and bred in the San Francisco Bay Area, and we begin to see certain historical forces colliding, but also generating, the other guy, the dude who is many things at once, but averse to definition from the external. He's more suited to avatars, Facebook pages and the remote, distanced logics of texting and tweeting. Thinking again about the Old Spice men—somewhere in there there's a man in there–I want to argue for a conception of other guy subjectivity as inherently epistemologically split between subject and object, between interior and exterior. The maintenance and policing of these boundaries are part and parcel of contemporary media masculinity, to the extent that men think of their bodies as being defined as what is seen and what is not, what is witnessed and what is best ignored. Classic and obvious examples of this are men's stereotypical inability to visit the doctor or the dentist, to ask for directions, or see a psychologist to talk about their feelings. All of these are betrayals of an internality that must be self-sufficient, unspoken, and unquestioned. These two sites, of course, correspond (particularly in the Freudian sense) to the visibility of the penis and the 'invisibility' of the vagina, to the extent that the masculine body as site is always a series of signs that refer back to the penis as the referent/signifier that guarantees not only the viability of the body *in situ*, but the body itself as hierarchical system, one that functions like any language system, through predication (the internal functioning as a kind of grammar, the external as a kind of syntax). Additionally, the male body operates as a performative site, so that the internal spaces take the shape of subtext and subplot, while the external (particularly the more nominally 'masculine' parts of the male body— the muscles, the testicles, the penis) serve as a system of speech acts, as well as a staged and framed device. In this sense, the male can make sense of his 'acceptable' risks in relation to other subjects and objects—is this other male a threat (subject) or is he an ally? Is this female available as 'property' (object), or does she function as a subject and therefore a type of threat or conquest? A model such as this is fluid, with identity characteristics such as age, ethnicity, weight, height, shape, etc., factoring into how much of an internal or external emphasis is comprehended or performed, and similarly, how 'subjectifying' or objectifying he may be (moment to moment). Like the body map we've built, diagramming the male body is as important as visualizing or theorizing masculinity, and in a sense, is a re-charging of a kind of essentialism that moves away from the problems of philosophical origins and referents and how these can be (sometimes inevitably) enunciated through the partriarchy, but instead feels—pushes against—and draws out individual male bodies as always-already essentialized performances of both anxiety and violence.

Constructions of Masculinity

In Anne Fausto-Sterling's essay, "How to Build a Man," the scientific rhetoric of developmental biology is put on the chopping block in order to investigate its biases and the pernicious absence of neutrality or objectivity in various studies. Fausto-Sterling, a professor of medical science with a Ph.D. in developmental genetics, sets out to, "consider the truths that biologists extract from bodies, human and otherwise, to examine scientific accounts—some might even say constructions—of masculinity."[10] She reviews scientific literature that—well established since the 1920s—has shown that both sexes are constituted out of a single embryo and that both sexes' sexual organs are developed out of the indifferent fetal gonad, the originary tissue and structural source for genital development. This of course is followed by psychological development from birth through puberty and adolescence, ending with one of two possible outcomes: female or male. Fausto-Sterling identifies a particularly simplistic duality that is born out of the observation of these 'natural' pathways, as well as the underlying assumptions of the researchers themselves, that things are either 'normal' or 'abnormal,' and that, ironically, "biologists and physicians use natural biological variation to define normality. Armed with this description, they set out to eliminate the natural variation that gave them their definitions in the first place."[11] She points to the work of psychologist John Money (whom I will return to in a moment) as particularly influential—in a detrimental sense—to our understandings of human development. Fausto-Sterling describes the multi-step process of sexual differentiation during development, from chromosomal to hormonal to "sex of assignment and rearing," and then deftly calls attention to the all-mighty Y chromosome gene, particularly the language that researchers use to describe its functionality. Females, in the language of human development, are the default sex. They occur when the Master Sex-Determining Gene is absent; "A male embryo must activate its master gene and seize its developmental pathway from the underlying female ground plan."[12] A similar process occurs with the production of hormones, the presence of a particular hormone codes the male, while females develop through its absence. She then turns her attention to postnatal development, particularly when a baby boy is born with that most complex form of lack/absence, a penis that is too small. Common medical practice is to remove the penis so as not to hinder the male's 'normalness'—urinating standing up in order to fit in with other boys, sexual penetration upon reaching maturity, with the assumption a vagina is to be penetrated.

To put it bluntly, it seems that an imperfect female is a better choice than a male with too small a dick. Fausto-Sterling continues, touching on socialization and acculturation, particularly in Money's work and theories, ending with a conundrum as damning as it is insidious in its pseudo-progressiveness:

> Money makes a remarkable claim. Genetics and even hormones count less in making a man or a woman than does socialization. In sustaining that claim, his strongest evidence, his trump card is that the child born male but raised a female becomes a heterosexual female. In their accounts of the power of socialization, Money and his coworkers define heterosexual in terms of the sex of rearing. Thus, a child raised as a female (even if biologically male) who prefers male lovers is psychologically heterosexual, although genetically she is not.[13]

What is most important here is the manner in which certain scientists, particularly in the realm of developmental biology and genetics, pursue a diagnostic framework and surgical practice that supports and promotes heteronormativity while swaddling it in an approach that invalidates any kind of subconsciously driven behaviors, actions that come out of some form of person *inside* the person. Somewhere in there there's a man in there. Additionally, what about the lives of lesbians, gays, transgendered folks or anyone else avoiding this surgical, hormonal and genetic gamut, this inside/outside, subject/object dichotomy that appears to be 'natural' for many straight people?

In considering the bodies of other guys, of guys who are at least nominally destabilized by their own sense of lack or 'lessness,' I want to be clear to state that I am not advocating for a return to essentialist, centered subjectivity, throwing out acculturation in favor of biological determinism. What I am suggesting is that there can be a productive tension between the interplay of nature and nurture both critically and philosophically, as well as in the quotidian lives of men, that can also hold at bay any backsliding into essentialist discourse that precludes difference in favor of homogeneity, that addresses the post-postmodern anxieties and desires of mediatic forms of masculinity and men, particularly when it comes to the body. Additionally, it seems important to ask if indeed there is some percentile equation (50% nature, 50% nurture) that exists as a kind of target balance when critically analyzing gender and sexuality, and if this mélange in fact changes *over time* and in accordance to changes in the biological and social circumstances of men. Physical competition, so prevalent in the development and post-adolescence of most men is necessarily enacted differently when men's bodies age and begin to 'fail.'

A great deal of the other guy's crisis (and the crisis of white masculinity in general) circulates around the body's slow march toward inactivity, obsolescence and marginalization, to the extent that within other guyness a sense of the futility of working out, sports and careful attention to health is pervasive. This is illustrated by way of Paul Rudd's character in the Apatow films, or Jason Segal's in *The Five-Year Engagement*, where he succumbs to a kind of emasculated hibernation in the face of depression, all the while when dealing with his wife's successful career in the midst of the calamitous winters of the American Midwest, where he meekly succumbs to the darkness and cold through ice fishing, hunting and turning parts of deer and moose into household objects. Also, consider the wording of 'Somewhere in there there's a man in there.' The shape of the external male becomes less relevant than the place, the *where* in *there*, so that what's left for the other guy isn't a makeover à la *Queer Eye for the Straight Guy*, but a reinvigoration of his masculinity inside himself, something deeper than the body and the higher functions of the mind, something somewhere in his primal resources, his gut instincts, his reptilian 'think meat.' It seems clear that everyday men still believe strongly in a central self, something inside the body that can be expressed through the body (the muscles, particularly), but aging throws this into question, so that as the man ages, a recalcitrant adherence to masculine rules (the biggest guy in the room still calls the shots, although occasionally age is still respected) and the travails of competition, breadwinning and sexual conquest (thanks to Viagra and Cialis). As I write this, House Republicans and the White House are locked in a game of chicken over the Affordable Care Act (which was passed as a law and upheld by the Supreme Court), resulting in a shutdown of the federal government, including food subsidies for single mothers and children, amongst other vital national services and departments. A senior Obama administration official opined, "We are winning…It doesn't really matter to us" how long the shutdown lasts, "because what matters is the end result."[14] Using the rhetoric of games, sports and competition is typical of news agencies and has become standard issue in American politics. As they age, men tend to overcompensate for their sagging flesh and atrophied muscles with discourse that continuously relies on metaphors from sports or battle, as if to reassert the man somewhere in there. The fact that President Obama's physique is that of a young man—lithe, fit and tall, while also being of African descent—most certainly serves as the most painful kind of insult/rebuke to a white, silver-haired patrician senator from the South. So, this leads me to an important point about male bodies; to understand masculinity one must always consider and unpack those around him, their level of difference, their relative size and age, and how the aggregate operates as a constant and dynamic threat matrix, challenging each man's notion of their self-worth in the most concrete of forms—how they size up.

Alpha/Beta/Omega—The New Masculine Hierarchy

While the term 'alpha male' dates back decades within various scientific disciplines (particularly in ethology), a new hierarchy of everyday masculinity has enunciated itself within the last decade or so in what can be termed the 'alpha-beta-omega-male debates,' namely who they are, what defines each level and what this in turn says about our current attitudes toward masculinity (and therefore politics, the economy, women, culture at large, etc.). This rhetoric has become highly visible throughout pop culture, winding its way into films like *A.C.O.D.* (Adult Children of Divorce) and the slacker, coming-of age comedy *True Adolescents* (again, featuring Mark Duplass, the go-to guy for the other guy in 'kidulthood'), as well as TV shows like the uncommonly solid and prescient (and ruefully, canceled) *Men of a Certain Age*, the painfully unfunny and derivative sitcom *We Are Men*, and the ABC Family sitcom *Baby Daddy*, a kind-hearted, family-friendly version of *Two and a Half Men*. A 2006 Reihan Salam article, "Masturbation and Solitude: The Adam Sandler Production That Will Save Mankind," is the first printed use of the term "beta male" in the popular press, and also serves as the first example of an 'answer' to the epistemological dominance of the alpha male concept in the popular press and consciousness, and to an extent, in the study of masculinity itself as a strategy (particularly in business and management theory).[15] In an insightful and funny 2010 article in *Slate* entitled, "Omega Males and the Women Who Hate Them," author Jessica Grose offers Ben Stiller's character in the Noah Baumbach cringe-comedy *Greenberg* as an omega man *par excellence*. In the film, Greenberg is middle-aged, angry, bitter, smug and beaten, and this is clearly his own doing, yet he wears it as armor, shielding him from the world of sincerity. Recalling the work of Susan Faludi, particularly her 1999 book *Stiffed: The Betrayal of the American Man*, Grose writes that,

> The image of the American woman has gone through several upheavals since the 1950s, but the masculine ideal seems fixed in cultural aspic: Think slick ad executive Don Draper in *Mad Men* and WWII heroes in the Tom Hanks-produced HBO series *The Pacific*. So his confused, paralyzed counterpart is cropping up in ever-more variations on TV and in movies: the omega male.[16]

Grose even divides these omega males into subspecies; the "Liberal Layabout," (failed, bitter artists and literary types), the "mimbo" (the male bimbo who *doesn't* use his looks to gain favor, as that would involve effort), "Beer Guy" (staple of Super Bowl/Bud Light ads, subdivided into "Original Beer Guy" and "Sad Beer Guy"—the sad version used to be fun, but middle age has beaten him down), and the "Game Boy" (after the portable videogame device; the perpetual adolescents). Grose, using corporate parlance, likens the alpha male to the CEO, the beta male to the middle manager (her example is Jim Halpert from the TV show, *The Office*), and the omega male to an unemployed slacker who has opted out of the whole damn thing. Additionally, she points out that, "The omega male is not experiencing the tired trope of the midlife crisis. A midlife crisis implies agency, a man who has the job and the family and chooses to reject it. The omega male doesn't have the power to reject anything—he's the one who has been brushed off." So, here we see several issues masquerading as a critique of a particular masculine failure or crisis. First, Grose is enunciating a larger cultural malaise, where the straight (Grose seems to only be speaking about white, straight men) male archetypes of the past (she uses Don Draper from *Mad Men* as an example) are both impossible to live up to for contemporary men but also too rooted in traditions of patriarchal privilege and prestige to function as an effective model, particularly for more progressive women (and, presumably, men). Second, certain forces (cultural, economic, social) have left men with fewer options to achieve a status that would afford them the means to *reject* traditional sexism and misogyny in a meaningful manner. Third, Grose criticizes omega males for opting out, for not taking a more proactive role in maintaining gainful employment and, most importantly, for not rejecting current social trends where (largely digitized) individualist expression has morphed into narcissistic self-documentation and masturbatory self-promotion. However, her position insinuates that this kind of behavior would be looked upon more favorably if women were doing it, to the extent that the categories that Grose has devised serve as a very conservative body of criticism of the other guy, first and foremost because he is engaging in 'feminine' (or at least 'un-masculine') behavior. After all, as the classic chauvinist stereotype goes, women are chatty, catty and shallow, what with their scrapbooks, knitting circles and book clubs. What, then, are these omega males doing, with their beauty products, online multiplayer videogames and Woody Allen-esque film knowledge, if not hijacking the psychology, social tactics and domestic spaces that belong to women? Writing articulately about the various hierarchies of men that are in part products of the increased exposure of others to men's anxieties and failings through increased dialogue in the popular media, Grose still falls prey to the trap that she disdains, a trap that is so pervasive that its often unacknowledged as a problem in itself—the assumptive power of masculinity as rooted in corporeal and psychological stereotypes that continuously prop up the strong, silent type, even if it is in the shape of a contemporary feminist popular discourse that seeks to undo so much of what passes as 'progressive' masculinity. So, while the omega men that Grose describes undeniably exist in the real and on the screen, these men are, in a pretty exacting sense, rejecting the kind of macho stereotypes against which all men are still too often measured. Unfortunately, the discourse of 'earning power' and its rejection by some omega males is part of the broader, new-male experiment, and in Grose's article, these men's 'choices' are propped up by certain feminine expectations, so that the concept of the male 'provider' still retains its stranglehold on the women who are actively dismantling and shucking this masculine position off in actual, lived domestic, public and work spaces. This is in no means an apologetics for lazy men, nor should it be read as making light of the real suffering that unemployed or bullied men endure, as well as the effects it has on their families. It is, however, in line with the nightly news stories that ask, "What happens to men when their wives make more than them?" a question that, yet again, casts men as victims and women as overstepping their roles. As Sally Robinson writes in her astute book *Marked Men*, "Making a virtue out of necessity, the wounded white male stakes a claim to an entire set of cultural conventions originally designed to identify those bodies and subjectivities made to suffer so that white men could retain privileged access to a disembodied norm."[17] The question here is how is this hierarchy a symptom of potential female complicity in male victimhood, even if this position is ostensibly critical of particular forms of masculinity? It's significant to note that the use of Greek letters (Alpha, Beta, Omega…) is itself a perpetuation of a classical intellectual hierarchy, albeit inaccurately. In the Greek alphabet, Alpha and Beta are followed by Gamma, not Omega. Omega is the last letter of this alphabet, or the ultimate limit of a set, and so this intimates that Omega males are, in fact, lesser than *20 other levels* of masculinity. If this was the purpose of choosing Omega, perhaps omicron would have been more descriptive, as Omega also means 'great O,' whereas omicron means 'little o,' a useful denotation if one wants to emphasize these 'last' men as small, physically or comparatively. In this sense, then, the other guy may best be described as the Delta man, as Delta is often used in mathematics and science to describe change, where Delta is the initial letter of the Greek word, *diaphorá*, or difference.

In November of 2012, author and pop psychologist Suzanne Venker ("Writer. Speaker. Truth-teller."), founder of WFM (Women For Men, "an organization committed to the needs of boys and men and to bringing the sexes together") penned an article for FoxNews.com entitled, "The War on Men." Opening with statistics from a recent Pew Research Center poll, Venker states that the number of women ages 18–34 who say that marriage is one of the most important aspects of their lives has actually increased since 1997 from 28 to 37 percent, while men have showed, in similar numbers, a drop in interest in marriage. The reason, she writes, isn't that men have changed, instead "women aren't women anymore."

> In a nutshell, women are angry. They're also defensive, though often unknowingly. That's because they've been raised to think of men as the enemy. Armed with this new attitude, women pushed men off their pedestal (women had their own pedestal, but feminists convinced them otherwise) and climbed up to take what they were taught to believe was rightfully theirs. Now the men have nowhere to go. It is precisely this dynamic—women good/men bad—that has destroyed the relationship between the sexes. Yet somehow, men are still to blame when love goes awry. Heck, men have been to blame since feminists first took to the streets in the 1970s.[18]

Venker's position here seems to be a brand of edgy, progressive anti-feminism, but I like to argue that it's something more, what I call 'inverse feminism.' Venker is taking a stance against feminism while simultaneously propping men up *while also* turning them into victims of feminism, as a means of creating a new feminine politics, one based on blaming women for pursuing feminism not as a response to the patriarchy, sexism and oppression, but in response to women like her, real women who follow what is in their "DNA." She ups the ante yet again in the article when she claims that, "Feminism serves men very well: they can have sex at hello and even live with their girlfriends with no responsibilities whatsoever." This is a half-clever trick in that it blames women who have turned feminism into a kind of lifestyle-opportunism, while letting guys off the hook for, again, just following their genetic pre-dispositions. Who knew feminism was cooked up for a man's benefit all along? So, as Grose fairly calls certain styles of other guy out on their peacocking and lethargy, Venker gives us a 'fair and balanced' diagnosis for what ails the other guy (and the sexes in general): "So if men today are slackers, and if they're retreating from marriage en masse, women should look in the mirror and ask themselves what role they've played to bring about this transformation." However, in a final, sweeping and circuitous leap of logic, Venker writes, "Fortunately, there is good news: women have the power to turn everything around. All they have to do is surrender to their nature—their femininity— and let men surrender to theirs." Thus, feminism, and by extension that hard-earned power that women have fought for, is, quite literally, best put to use in maintaining the old codes of power. Women now have the choice to use their empowerment to disempower themselves, opting for the kitchen and the crib over the community and a corner office. For Venker and her reactionary allies' minds, it seems that the other guy is also partially to blame—his delay of a mature life of marriage and kids, while also choosing to surreptitiously acknowledge women as partners and equals, serves as a form of dissociative disorder, brought on by the feminist infection and its attendant social and political symptomology.

A few days after Venker wrote "The War on Men," (truth be told, it served as a promotion/précis for her book *The War on Men*, published in early 2013), Michael Kimmel responded with "The Mythical 'War on Men,'" posted on CNN.com.[19] Beginning with an appearance Kimmel made during the past year on a talking-heads news show entitled, "A black woman stole my job," Kimmel initiated his response to Venker's article by highlighting an important word in the title of the segment, "my." His aim was to draw attention to the notion that the "four angry white men" that appeared on the show had settled into the trap of entitlement. These jobs were, after all, supposed to be 'their' jobs, as was most everything out there, in the workplace and in life. Kimmel writes,

> I thought of those men recently while reading Suzanne Venker's addled rant against feminist women as the source of the unhappiness that saturates male-female relation-ships. I thought of how painful it is when you are used to having everything to now have only 80%. What a loss! Poor us! Equality sucks when you've been on top—and men have been on top for so long that we think it's a level playing field.[20]

He continues by addressing Venker's obfuscation of the roots of feminism, noting that the 'good woman/bad man' trope served as the cradle of anti-feminism, instead of as Venker would have it, the *source* of feminism, where a woman's primary job was to soothe the savage beast and reign in her man by way of her natural, essential, mollifying powers. Crass essentialism notwithstanding, he notes that of the 400 men he interviewed for his book, *Guyland,* most of them acknowledged that their female partners' jobs would be as important to them, as would theirs be to their partners. "Why? Because they'll need the income. And they assume, with no resentment, that they will be involved fathers, spending far more time with their families than their parents or grandparents ever did. Why? Because they actually want to be involved dads." Again, the notions of entitlement, gender roles and inequality become earmarks for a larger culture war, one clearly substantiated by the election of Barack Obama and changing demographics in the U.S. Suzanne Venker is, much like the *Newsweek* magazine cover above bemoaning "The Beached White Male," looking for a scapegoat for the relative dissolution of male privilege. And, while Venker seems to think it's women, Kimmel artfully refashions the conflict, away from a war between the sexes, toward equality and equanimity, one that I argue the other guy is attempting (often through debates between himself and his male friends) to articulate, albeit too often in a defeatist tone. As Kimmel declares at the end of his response, "Venker paints a most unyieldingly awful portrait of men, one that is happily belied by actual, real, American men. And we won't stand for the sort of male-bashing Venker offers. We want it all also—and the only way we can have it all is to halve it all." In the end, the other guy is willing to share, go dutch and help out, but often misunderstands that apportioning the tools doesn't necessarily mean relinquishing them completely. However, real, tangible progress will happen when the other guy realizes that he had access to the tools in the first place.

It is important to note that after initial reaction to her statements, Venker apologized for the uproar, claiming that she meant to write about husbands and wives, instead of men and women. She spoke with the *Daily Beast*, saying;

> All I can say in my defense is that it can be so hard when you write as much as I've written—three books, articles, blogs—you think you have said something but you haven't. It's like I am thinking something and I am so clear about it and I think what I have said is that. I don't know. I don't know. I didn't think that much about it. It is an important distinction between men and husbands for sure.[21]

It is illuminating that Venker went on to say that it would be easy to misinterpret her position, and the article, as the statements she made were "open-ended." Venker, in not understanding at the most basic level that commentary or theory of gender is itself open-ended, largely because the dynamic nature of gender formation and accrual can itself be self-delusional (particularly in hyper- or alpha masculinity) and highly contingent, makes an error that speaks directly to conservative notions of gender roles. In her failure of imagination to account for the diversity of attitudes and behaviors of men and women,

Venker in a sense, relinquishes her own ability to apologize, for that would fly in the face of her essentialist and ossified categorization of gender roles. The fact that she did and (I think) sincerely tried to address valid concerns, is an excellent sign that even the most reactionary must acknowledge the act of interpretation as essential to discourse, and therefore to gender roles themselves. More sinisterly, she could be only nominally apologizing as a means of capitulating to her role as subjugated woman, a learned subservience that calls for apologies when none are necessary. Or, she could be just trying to sell books, supplicating herself as so many of us do to a digitally driven marketplace still owned and operated by men.

Humor, Satire, and Camp:
The Other Guy Makes a Funny

Consisting of Akiva Schaffer, Andy Samberg and Jorma Taccone, The Lonely Island is a comedy group that satirizes pop culture through music and music videos, initially finding success on *Saturday Night Live*, particularly in their 'digital shorts.' Citing Steve Martin, Mel Brooks and the Monty Python troupe as influences, their work has achieved viral status on YouTube (one of their videos has reached 100 million views), and have earned them Grammy and Emmy nominations, chiefly because of their uncanny ability to skewer the zeitgeist in a manner that seems both inclusive and self-effacing. "I think self-deprecation is a big part of our humor," Taccone says. "I still occasionally die laughing just thinking that my name is Jorma. Like, that's really funny."[22] Their work is also embraced by pop music heavyweights; Justin Timberlake, Lady Gaga, Snoop Dogg and Michael Bolton have performed on their songs and in their videos, as have actors Natalie Portman, Will Ferrell and Jessica Alba, resulting in parodies of the stars themselves, as well as their music and careers. So, in a sense, they are extensions of SNL's general satirical oeuvre, while also working as a counter-cultural rejoinder to the hyper-exposure and cult of the star amplified by/in the digital age. A recent song, YOLO, works as a send-up of the shallow exuberance of the original meme 'yolo' (you only live once), a clarion call of young hipsters convinced they need to 'carpe the diem' and capture their hijinks on SnapChat, Vine or Facetime. Instead of 'you only live once,' however, The Lonely Island repurposed it into 'you oughta look out,' detailing numerous ways kids can meet an early demise, while recommending smart financial planning and a hyper-vigilant, safe and solitary lifestyle. In addition to love, hip-hop, teenagers, racial stereotypes and food, The Lonely Island is particularly interested in critiquing various forms of masculinity while consistently identifying with an other guy sensibility. Their anfractuous lyrics create an ironic, paradoxical and absurdist positionality that often ups the ante on masculine stereotypes in order to create a Beckettesque loop of mistake and apology, action and retraction, enunciation and confusion. In the song "The Compliments," a dub-step send-up with electronica elements, the three take turns admiring each other, while old school rapper Too $hort comments on their bromance during refrains. Eventually, the praise turns sexual and Too $hort, playing the atypical homophobic rapper, ends the song warning women that The Lonely Island love themselves more than anyone else. What is useful here is the laundry list of other guy objects, pursuits and attitudes: they cook each other brunch, make great "skinny margaritas," have good dental hygiene and aren't "afraid of a broom." Contrast these quotidian other guy admirations with loyalty so great that they only think of each other when masturbating, and now we're approaching a high point in the low theory of masculinity—where masculinity has been drawn back into itself in the form of self-preservation, 'manscaping,' and bromance, so that other male bodies and selves are the natural sexual and desiring object. They'll seemingly do anything to avoid women—while at the same time embracing an adoptive straight-gayness in yet another surreptitious cooptation of polyvocality, as well as a reassertion of their nostalgic univocality. Commenting on how they are, at least nominally, progressive males, Akiva Shaffer stated,

> There was a moment where I, under my breath at one point, called my mother a 'b——' and my mother hit me so hard, and shook me, and looked me in the eye and said, 'Don't ever say that word about a woman ever in your life. It's the most insulting thing you could possibly say to a woman.' And then I remember my brother, years later, did the exact same thing, under his breath, called her a 'b——,' and then she tried to go there with him and he said, 'I said witch! Oh my god!' And he tricked her, and I was like, 'Oh younger kids are just smarter.' But because of that, I never say that word ever. I find it very insulting.[23]

They continue to cleverly unpack masculine sexual desire and negotiation in the song "No Homo," a commentary on the parenthetical insertion of 'no homo' or 'pause' used by straight men (particularly in the black and hip-hop community) to qualify themselves as 'not gay' after saying something that might be construed as 'gay.' The music and sonic texture of the song resembles heavier, darker hip-hop styles, with roots in Public Enemy or Tupac Shakur. Again, The Lonely Island works from a place of relative familiarity and stability, establishing (masculine) rules for the song:

> When you want to compliment a friend (no homo)
> But you don't want that friendship to end (no homo)
> So tell a dude just how you feel (no homo)
> Say 'no homo' so he knows the deal (no homo)

The (no homo) utterance, musically, is composed of a chorus of voices, sampled and then inserted after each line, resulting in a repetitive, habituated declaration of hyper-hetero presence. These outwardly simple rules are quickly followed by increasingly transgressive statements, so that the (no homo) begins to deform into a more virulent denial, an "Am I right!?" followed by a punch in the arm or a slap on the butt. And yet, the (no homo) lyric remains an unemotional chant because of its sampled nature. Hence while the declaratives and questions become more heated, it is they that take on additional signifying force *because* of (no homo)'s apparent sameness;

> I like the way your shoulders fill out that shirt (no homo)
> It's hard to pull off but you make it work (no homo)
> Hey yo I kinda like your natural scent (no homo)
> Hey yo I kinda like the musical Rent (no homo)

And then progressing to;
> Yo we should watch this gay porno tape (no homo)
> but as a joke because we're all straight (no homo)
> man you could wash laundry on those abs (no homo)
> Yo I think girls look good in drag (no homo)
> Hey yo I've been thinking about posing nude (no homo)
> Hey yo I've been thinking about fuckin a dude (no homo)

Ending with;
> Hey no homo but today I'm coming out the closet
> and I scream it from the mountains like a gay prophet
> those two words have set me free (no homo)
> damn it feels good to be (no homo)

This last quatrain reveals the end game, a homophobia transformed into a clarion call of self-realization and freedom. Because of the juxtaposition between the opening and the ending, the inherent denial and affirmation of the phrase 'no homo,' the protagonist has paradoxically been enabled to come out of the closet, yet only to the extent that we are uncertain whether he is 'feeling good' about re-affirming his heteronormativity, and therefore his homophobia. The Lonely Island appears to operate between the excesses of both the parodic celebration of über-masculinity and the primped, sensitive metrosexual, probing the interstices of masculine self-depreciative humor. "We're tiny white dudes," as Andy Samberg concisely states, tossing their bodies and attendant vestiges of self-esteem onto a bonfire of fast-evaporating power.

Queer Eye and Transformative Consumerism

Saturday Night Live, the space where The Lonely Island's work first surfaced, has for more than three decades reflected the motley discourse of New York City and its historical sexual transgressiveness (Stonewall, Studio 54, The Velvet Underground, etc.). Yet, a network stalwart like *Saturday Night Live* speaks a great deal about the cultural influence of the city itself as well as the artists that work there, while representing the city itself to the rest of the country as both a multicultural city-on-the-edge as well as a space of blue-state liberal excess, filth and crisis. With this as a background, one must consider two important, yet seemingly unrelated, historical and cultural events and how they helped shape modern masculinity in the U.S.: the 9/11 attacks and *Queer Eye for the Straight Guy*. In no way shape or form do I wish to diminish the tragic events of September 11 by juxtaposing it with a reality TV show like *Queer Eye*. I do, however, want to suggest that both represent conflicting attitudes within and around masculinity in the first decade of the 21st century.

In *The Media and Modes of Masculinity*, Mark Moss writes, "Since September 11, 2001, it has been suggested that "manhood" is once again being held in high esteem. With the return of the traditional male heroes—firemen, policemen, soldiers—a renewed emphasis on "going back" has been in vogue. The return of the honest hero as a character and type resonates throughout culture and media."[24] Moss finds that a return to these kinds of masculine types is partially to blame for the prolonged immaturity in men, in that harkening back to these kinds of bodies and attitudes—heroic, physical, regimented—functions as a delaying tactic in the face of more complex cultural and historical contingencies, particularly feminism. Gary Cross makes similar arguments throughout his book, *Men to Boys: The Making of Modern Immaturity*. Additionally, possibly the most complicated masculinity caught on camera in the aftermath of the 9/11 attacks was Rudy Giuliani, then mayor of New York City. Diminutive in stature, but with a bulldog's tenacity, Giuliani was simultaneously lauded and criticized for his efforts during the attacks and in the ensuing devastation, particularly considering how often he was on camera. In the end, he was given Person of the Year by *Time Magazine*. What is important here is the way that Giuliani transformed his masculinity from an abrupt, domineering and calculating pol into a man who better mirrored the first responders—regular guys who showed a quiet and restrained ethos of togetherness, often in a heroic manner. So, the 'little-big guy' performed a more salient masculinity for a city (and a geographic area) that is symbolized by men with thick accents and blue-collar jobs, cynically mocked by the goons on *Jersey Shore*. Now, I would like to, as Moss does, juxtapose this with *Queer Eye for the Straight Guy* as a means of finding the other guy's local flavor in the five boroughs.

Moss begins his discussion by focusing on the metrosexual and his two historical antecedents, the dandy and the *flaneur*, in order to sketch out the root of the new male vanity as a reaction to the modern world. Walter Benjamin's descriptions of the *flaneur* are key here, as he emphasized the urban wanderer's place in the world as one primarily born out of the significant changes in urban planning and use wrought by the transformation of the bourgeoisie's tastes toward consumption.[25] The *flaneur*, however, was also a function of a new mobility and visibility, particularly in relation to spaces of visual consumption—the Paris Arcades, in Benjamin's famous example—with the ability to move in and around these spaces in a meandering and dreamlike state, with the new virtual mobility of the cinema working as a subconscious ignition for visual desires. Additionally, a self-regarding dimension was essential to the *flaneur*—he was *to be seen* as much as he was *to see*, similar to other performing, decidedly self-conscious, masculinities throughout the ages, from the saturnalian festivities at the court of Louis XIV (particularly when male members of court would sit on stage *while* a play was staged) to what Steven Cohan has fabulously termed the "age of the chest"—the constantly on-display chests of men in the movies during the 1950s (Kirk Douglas, Steve Reeves, Charlton Heston, etc.) or the *peplum* films of the same era.[26] So, the *flaneur* serves as a rehearsal for the postmodern male-as-pure-image, to the degree that what we see in film, on TV, in videogames, print, and on the Internet had a kind of inevitability when *Queer Eye for the Straight Guy* started critiquing, repairing and sublimating the other guy (again, the inevitable masculine type for this show—certainly also an other guy's acknowledgment of his own cluelessness).

A typical episode of *Queer Eye*[27] finds the Fab Five—Ted, Thom, Jai, Kyan and Carson (who each have a specialty area—food and beverage, fashion, grooming, interior design, etc.) looking through a file about their 'subject,' a straight male in need of a life makeover (except for three particular episodes, where they trained their sights on two gay men and a transgender person). They fix his clothes, take him to the salon, teach him to make a meal (often for his wife or girlfriend) and usually finish off with a 'reveal' for the spouse: a freshly groomed and sharply dressed man, with a special meal laid out on hip new dinner ware, surrounded by a redesigned room. This material is interspersed with shots the Fab Five viewing footage of the subject (while they munch on sumptuous snacks and delicious drinks), in a fascinating combination of voyeuristic and scopophilic pleasure, cheering him on when he succeeds, tsk-tsking him when he doesn't listen to their advice. Our pleasure, the audience's, is therefore reliant on our presumption that gay men's fashion, design and physical taste is superior to that of the average straight guy. It is, after all, *Queer Eye for the Straight Guy*, so that straight men may see the world *through their eyes* in a way they never have before, a reflection of the longstanding stereotype that gay men seem to have it all (despite the economic disparities between average middle-class straight men and gay men). Yet, while the straight man may seem to have undergone a transformation, what has really happened is a common consumerist fantasy—access has been granted to free goods and services paid for by the show, so that the subject-male finds himself in a moment of blissful transcendence, catapulted out of his class anchorages. So, what do we say about the other guy, the straight guy at the heart of the gay male gaze and manipulation? What slyly happens here is an example of men's acknowledgment of the changing nature of the modern world, instead of just simple indulgence in a vanity project. This is witnessed in the way each straight guy in each episode reacts to each of the Fab Five's suggestions and advice, often in the form of an addict facing sobriety: surprise, confusion, denial, bargaining, and finally with the 'reveal' and the adulation of their partner, acceptance. This process is textbook other guy—he puts up half a fight when it comes to alterations in his masculine behavior and attitudes, mostly for show, eventually admitting defeat in a manner that hints at 'progress.' Additionally, the show is set and shot in New York, and yet we manage to only see nice streets with nice shops and nice salons, the Fab Five driving around in a brand-new SUV that seems immune to midtown traffic or rabid cabbies. The effect sells the city as much as its services, effectively erasing the pain of 9/11, the urban poor and homeless, the ethnic tensions that follow gentrification of traditional neighborhoods, as well as the more typical tough-guy masculinity so often associated with the city (the New York men of Scorsese's films, for instance). And then there are the women, partners of each straight guy. Bemoaning either the old days when he seemed to care, or his present lack of initiative, they are immediately cast as the 'fag hag' when the Fab Five listen intently and coo their sympathies (implying that all straight women could do with a few gay male friends), eventually driven to tears when they see their beau transformed. The effect is mixed; the straight guys are celebrated for their open-mindedness and lack of homophobia, the Fab Five are feted for their highly evolved (but wearingly trivial) lifestyles, and the women are cast as both victim and savior through their teary-eyed revelation that this man, this straight guy is, after all, a good lug, and therefore the right choice. The other guy is like a run-down mid-century modern, his charm isn't in his present 'curb-appeal,' it's in his solid foundation and potential as a fixer-upper.

Dickwolves, Gender and Gamer Culture

While I have focused on the physical presence of the other guy for the bulk of this chapter, I would be remiss if I didn't include an inspection of the other guy's virtual presence, particularly in the world of videogames. For the other guy, videogames are a central text, activity and space; studies show that men born between 1970 and 1990 are the heaviest users of console and PC videogames, heavier even than their younger counterparts, who seem more interested in mobile gaming and social networking. This includes MMOGs (Massive Multiplayer Online Games) such as *World of Warcraft*, but also FPS's (First Person Shooters), the *Call of Duty* franchise for example, adventure games like the *Grand Theft Auto* series, as well as more physically active games offered by the Wii and xBoxKinect systems (including play zones like the Dave & Buster's chain of adult arcades). However, a great deal of time and work in the discipline of games studies has been devoted to studying the behavior and culture of online gaming, and at nearly a decade and a half, games studies has matured into a discipline with its own methodologies and debates, many of which stem from the more sociologically based study of online gaming. Harald Warmelink and Marko Siitonen's recent article details in *Journal of Games and Virtual Worlds*, "A Decade of Research into Player Communities in Online Games," details this exegesis. In the article, the authors identify three major group divisions: *micro* (player groups), *meso* (guilds), and *macro* (communities), as well as six different aspects and operationalizations of player groups, "culture and social norms, social structuring, rationale, number of members, used information and communication technologies, and time of existence."[28] These six aspects have been used consistently and methodically in MMOG research in the past decade. However, the bulk of the debates have focused on the first attribute, culture and social norms, particularly in relation to player group self-aggregation and the institution of rules and social mores.[29] This feature is, arguably, the most complex and polyvalent, as it has a distinct and clear relationship to the gamers not only as avatars/characters in game space, but as players themselves, people who live and breathe gaming out in non-gamespace and who often breach the "magic circle," or the inclusive communities comprised of serious gamers.[30] Often, the distinction between their lives as gamers and their lives as avatars within an online community merge in the form of face-to-face conventions, online forums, blogs and other extensions of the game world, like table-top RPGs (Role Playing Games), LARPing (Live Action Role Playing; narratively based, theatrical and ritualized performance), or cosplay (where fans dress up as their object of identification in public using elaborate costumes and makeup). However, relatively little has been written on gaming and masculinity, whether it's in the representative politics in the stories, characters or scenarios, within the communities in online worlds, or within and around gamer groups on the Web. In my previous book, *Die Tryin': Videogames, Masculinity, Culture*, I argue that a great deal of the digital imaginary is predicated on 'boyhood,' or the regressive state of masculinity engendered by gaming and game culture, so that the player is hailed as a joystick jockey, a digital boy interested in a relatively narrow set of texts, behaviors and attitudes (although the average age of the male gamer is around 30).[31] Yet, in the past decade, more and more women have engaged with gaming, with one study by the Electronic Software Association finding that women comprise 45% of the active game audience, with women over 18 comprising 30% of the game playing community, whereas boys under 17 only comprise 18%.[32]

As a gamer and a digital dude, the other guy often associates with and engages in online gaming, although it is not a prerequisite for other guyness—some other guys eschew gaming because of its longstanding signifiers of overt adolescence, sexism and violence, as well as the cultural stereotypes that identify the gamer as a poorly socialized recluse. As I've mentioned before, the other guy is a synaesthetic masculinity, one built of many styles, interests and behaviors, so if he does play games, signs point to online play, as well as social play, as the other guy is a social creature (albeit a great deal of that socializing is networked or digital). What I would like to focus on in this section is a strange outgrowth of the collision between digital masculinity and feminism and women in online communities, particularly in the online gamer community. What we'll see as this narrative/debate is traced out is just how unwilling many guys—including other guys—are to let women into the "magic circle" of games and gaming (as well as the 'magic box' of game development), and how strains of sexism, misogyny and rape culture are still hallmarks of not only geek/gamer culture, but that an explosive contradiction exists between the old rhetoric of hegemonic masculinity and digital 'boyhood' that creates an inclusive, myopic community that is deeply resistant and resentful of women, virtual and real. Arguably, because much of the debates of the Dickwolves saga happened online, the familiar brand of (semi) anonymous, digital bravado is ubiquitous. However, the central reason I draw attention to this debate is to highlight the dangers that the other guy (as well as all men) face when it comes to digital spaces and communities, chiefly how the acknowledgment of the socially constructed nature of gender can fall victim to the backsliding and destructive vicissitudes of the essentialized body and all the rights 'guaranteed' therein to men's bodies. What is particularly alarming here is that these digital men, these gamers and world makers, who often identify themselves as virulently non-macho and un-hyper-masculine, can perform the same old tricks, as long as there's a captive audience and his buddies to pat him on the back (or the butt).

Penny Arcade, a webcomic and portal that (as of 2010) had nearly 3.5 million readers, has been regularly generated since 1998. The strip's creators, writer Jerry Holkins and illustrator Mike Krahulik, have also created and manage PAX (an annual gaming convention, arguably the largest in North America), Child's Play (a charity that donates games and toys to children in hospitals), as well as tie-in videogames and other game-related art. It is safe to say that these two men are 'taste-makers' in the gaming world, both in the gamer community as well as the design community, and what they have to write, make and say is taken seriously, if not with adoration from many in both communities. The trouble began on August 11, 2010, when the site published "The Sixth Slave," wherein an NPC (Non-Player Character) urgently pleads with a player to save him from being raped nightly by beasts called "Dickwolves," monsters with phalluses for feet. To put this in context, players in MMOGs are often admonished to complete tasks or go on specific quests, such as 'free five slaves' or 'rescue the princess.' So, in this comic, the NPC is part of an imaginary game's code (and part of a particular quest), but being the "Sixth Slave," the player is not required to free him as a part of this imaginary quest. After the slave continues his pleas, the 'hero' says, "Hey. Pal. Don't make this weird." The joke here is referring to several things (and not just the annoyances of seemingly pointless, arbitrary quests), most particularly that rape is funny and that since the slave has already been raped—and therefore penetrated—he is clearly less than 'male,' hence the hero asking him to 'not make this weird,' which presumably means that the hero's masculinity would be called into question for even *acknowledging* the rape of another man as a distinct possibility. What followed over the next three years is fairly emblematic of the regressive, misogynistic attitudes of some gamers, how the gaming community circles the wagons when it comes to their 'turf,' but also how, over the span of three years, men themselves are capable of learning empathy, understanding and responsibility, albeit under pressure, as well as how many male and female gamers care about how their community operates and that inclusiveness and empathy can be central tenets. Additionally, it was through many other guys—synaesthetic men who are capable of weighing their needs and views against the needs of others through engagement of multiple positionalities and identities, through multiple media channels—can conceive of themselves as positive models that actively pursue a positive vision of men and masculinities.

Reaction to the comic was swift and energetic. On August 12, 2010, a guest blogger on the influential Shakesville site, a progressive feminist blog operating since 2004, commented that, "…a slave being raped is a real thing that happens in the world every day. I don't find this 'joke' funny because, unlike characters cartoonishly killing each other repeatedly and coming back to life, just as in video games, rape isn't a central feature of (most) games—at least in the actual gameplay, totally aside from the language used by players."[33] What followed on the next day were a series of responses from Holkins and Krohulik, most of them snarky, some of them belligerent, none of them apologetic. A back and forth followed, with significant comments from websites and web presences like the Geek Feminism blog, Game Politics, The Daily Cartoonist, Pretty Gamer and The Border House, along with a Tweet from Wil Wheaton, the actor who played Wesley Crusher on *Star Trek: The Next Generation* (who has also become a de facto geek guru and blogger, even appearing on *The Big Bang Theory* as himself), "Don't be a dickwolf," (Sept. 3, 2010). By this time, *Penny Arcade* had refused to concede that rape is a serious issue, regardless of the context, and they seemed to 'double-down' by offering Dickwolf t-shirts for sale through their online store. Then, in the late fall of 2010, as if on cue, *Penny Arcade* steered the discussion toward 'freedom of speech,' thus hijacking the true issue at hand—rape and rape jokes—by setting the debate up as a matter of censorship and political correctness. This should seem familiar to anyone who has followed the rise of majority group victim-narratives over the past decade, typically spun by whites, evangelical Christians, and/ or conservatives who are uncomfortable with an equitable, polyvocal culture, changing demographics in the U.S., or simply the perceived demonization of majority views and beliefs as *fiat*. As one commentator put it, "The argument was never that they shouldn't be allowed to make the joke, but that the critics wished that they were the types of people who wouldn't make the joke,"[34] indicating a wide-ranging set of views from members, producers, fans and outliers of this community, that gaming itself—and the gaming community by extension—has value, and can in fact, do better.

The ensuing and lengthy debate continued for weeks and months, with contributions and coverage from high-profile netizens and mainstream media outlets. Yet, the hurtful, callous and disturbing comments continued, with mentions of dickwolf-wearing flash mob gatherings and tweets such as this, posted February 22, 2011:

On September 11, 2012, the article, "Hypermasculinity & Dickwolves: The Contentious Role of Women in the New Gaming Public," appeared in the *Journal of Broadcasting and Electronic Media*, a comprehensive summary and theorization of the issues of sexism, gender identity and power at work in the *PA* debates, as well as on the web in general. The authors write that digital communication technologies create an air of (alleged) fairness and democracy, but that;

> …this is a mask behind which a form of gender essentialism hides which precipitates a harsh reprisal for any who dare to speak out about the dominant paradigm. Although the original gaming public's identity is based upon the outsider group mentality, their in-group dynamics have expanded upon women-hostile concepts of masculinity within the larger social sphere. This discourse, as amplified across social networks and in public online spaces, allows for extreme and virulent lashing out against those who are perceived as others, most notably women. Such silencing warps the seemingly social spaces of Web 2.0 into tools for the exclusion and perpetuation of a male-dominated gaming social public.

Additionally, at several academic gaming conferences that I attended from 2011 until the present, several panels were organized which included industry and design professionals in order to flesh out just what was at stake if online communities fail to make inclusiveness and empathy keystones, as well as what the gaming industry is doing in response to decades of male-dominated workplaces, sexist and misogynistic content, and how violence and hegemonic masculinity are often coupled together as natural cellmates. One particular conference, the 2013 Gotland Game Conference at Gotland

University in Sweden (which functions as an professional and academic conference, but also as a game design expo, as the university houses one of the most respected and influential game design programs in Europe, or the world, for that matter) was remarkable in that the focus of the conference was on gender, more particularly the problem of a male-dominated industry and an untapped and underserved female game design and player population. It was an inspiring and memorable event, with events and showcases in university buildings of striking design, meters from the cerulean waters of the Baltic Sea. The majority of the speakers were women, most from the game design industry, and most agreed that the current state of the industry was/is untenable if issues of gender equality and sexual inclusiveness are not addressed. However, the din of male designer voices was loud, often reactionary, and too often ready to respond without truly listening. These outbursts and tantrums were countered by the female and male academics, and by the female students (as well as quite a few male students) at the university, as well as from the female professionals and academics. And so a de facto progressive community was made in the midst of an ostensibly safe, equal (but still negotiated space), one where a small, vocal minority of the young male development students felt a) that gender inequity in games and game development wasn't a problem, b) that they certainly weren't part of the problem, and c) that games and game development are best left to the boys. But—*but!*—a strong majority of the young men that I met were not only interested, but dedicated, to fixing the problem. They had moved beyond *fight* or *flight*, and onto *fix*. A good sign, surely. These young men were other guys, the spitting image, with all of its complications. But, so were some of the other, angry male students. Most importantly, these young other guys were proud of own their sense—not of entitlement—but of empathy and compassion. And, they had the cognitive apparatus and emotional maturity to express this attitude, to me, a foreigner, in English, rather than in their native languages.

And so, conversely, many of the men that stood by the *Penny Arcade* creators continued to parade their entitled attitudes, reveling in an antique exclusionary masculinity. If not this, there still remains an air of 'I'm just a regular guy' tone to Krahulik and other commentators' continual denouncement of the issue as unimportant, not a gamer issue, not real. If there are apologies, they are hollow, a signal that they just want the problem to go away, and still don't truly understand the problem. Regrettably, Krahulik posted his support for a tentacle-rape card game and has made derogatory comments about the trans community throughout 2013. Some men refuse to learn. However, as the debate wore on—and it continues at the time of this writing—what has been remarkable, hopeful even, are the better strains of the other guy, the non-alphas—the deltas, if you will—who feel like their community is suffering because of what two men have done to their space, their shared history. Most surprisingly, one of those men perhaps capable of change is Mike Krahulik. The following is from his post entitled "Resolutions" on *PA*, Jan 1, 2014:

> I've learned a ridiculous amount this year. About myself and about other people. It's been a difficult year, probably the hardest in my life and I realize I brought most of it on myself. That's a sobering realization. I also realize that I've made it harder for the people I care about, my friends and my family. I can't be this guy anymore. I have every intention of taking the things I've learned this year to heart and changing. I've said sorry for the things I've said but I've never apologized for who I am. I need to separate the busted kid from the man I am now. I guess that's my new year's resolution. Might be harder than losing ten pounds.

If we take him at his word, this is a good example of what the other guy is capable of. And, it turns out that the vehicle for change was the community itself, and the responsibilities that came along with being a cultural producer, a voice for other guys. For the other guy, respecting yourself and your body, your contexts and roles, your partners, your children and friends, women and the LGBT community, is often a matter of reorienting the 'your' in favor of the 'our,' a shared, mutually imbricated masculine becoming, instead of one locked in perpetual struggle with himself and his surroundings.

Notes

1. The added 'h' in 'whimpy' is key, as its additional aspiration further represents this particular masculinity, and in this case, in the form of a more aerated illocution, a breathfull whisper/whimper in contradiction to the stereotypical masculine silence.
2. Anne Marie Chaker, "Groceries Become a Guy Thing, "As Men Shop More, Packaging Aims to Win Them Over; 'Inner Abs' Appeal" *WallStreetJournal.com*, Oct. 16, 2013.
3. Michael Kimmel, *Manhood in America: A Cultural History*, (New York: The Free Press, 1996), 292.
4. Kimmel, 294.
5. Raymond Williams, *Marxism and Literature*, 1977.
6. Kimmel, 300.
7. Kimmel, 309.
8. Kimmel, 317.

9. Michael Kaufman, "The Construction of Masculinity and the Triad of Men's Violence," in *Men's Lives*, 4th edition, Eds. Michael S. Kimmel and Michael A. Messner (Boston: Allyn and Bacon, 1998), 4–17.

10. Anna Fausto-Sterling, "How to Build a Man," in *Men's Lives*, 385.

11. Fausto-Sterling, 386.—John Colapinto, 'The True Story of John/Joan,' *Rolling Stone* December 1997: 54–97.—Money, John. (1988) *Gay, Straight, and In-Between: The Sexology of Erotic Orientation*. New York: Oxford University Press.

12. Fausto-Sterling, 386.

13. Ibid., 388.

14. Carol E. Lee and Peter Nicholas, "White House's Hard Line on Shutdown, Debt Ceiling Has Risks Attached," *The Wall Street Journal*, October 4, 2013.

15. Reihan Salam, "Masturbation and Solitude: The Adam Sandler Production That Will Save Mankind," *Slate*, May 19, 2006.

16. Jessica Grose, "Omega Males and the Women Who Hate Them," *Slate*, March 18, 2010.

17. Sally Robinson, *Marked Men*, 20.

18. Suzanne Venker, "The War on Men," *FoxNews.com*, November 26, 2012.

19. Michael Kimmel, "The Mythical 'War on Men,'" *CNN.com*, November 29, 2012.

20. Kimmel.

21. David Freedlander, "The War on Men Author Suzanne Venker, 'I'm Misunderstood!" *TheDailyBeast.com*, Nov. 27, 2013.

22. NPR.com, The Lonely Island: The Hottest Thing in Fake Hip-Hop, May 6, 2011.

23. *Fresh Air*, hosted by Terry Gross, "Samberg, Taccone and Schaffer: Three's Not a Lonely Island," *NPR* June 18, 2013.

24. Mark Moss, *The Media and Modes of Masculinity*, (Lexington, MD: Langham Books, 2011), 17.

25. See Walter Benjamin's unfinished magnum opus, *The Arcades Project*, or Susan Buck-Morse's creative and brilliant re-construction of it as a complete work, *The Dialectics of Seeing*.

26. See Steven Cohan, *Masked Men: Masculinity and the Movies in the Fifties*, (Bloomington, IN: Indiana U. Press, 1997), a brilliant, exhaustive and entertaining book. Of particular interest here is when and why the men's 'shaved chest' began to appear in films of the '50s, and how it signified as cinematic image, as an upheaval of the dichotomies of male/female, as well as a contrast to contemporary men in order to evoke a Greek or Roman classicism.

27. (Its original title, later adding the '*for the Straight Guy*' in season three, presumably to widen the audience, but also as an acknowledgment of just who might *already* be watching).

28. Harald Warmelink and Marko Siitonen, "A Decade of Research into Player Communities in Online Games," in *Journal of Gaming and Virtual Worlds*, Vol. 5:3, 2013, 271–293.

29. See Chan, M.G., "Communication, Coordination and Camaraderie in World of Warcraft," (*Games and Culture*, 4:1), C-Y Jang, "Managing Fairness: Reward Distribution in a Self-organized Online Game Player Community," in D. Schuler (ed.), *Proceedings of OCSC 2007: Online Communities and Social Computing* (Berlin: Springer-Verlag, 2007), or T.L. Taylor's excellent and provocative book, *Play between Worlds: Exploring Online Game Culture* (Cambridge, MA: MIT Press, 2006) for different examples of qualitative and quantitative approaches.

30. C. Pearce, *Communities at Play: Emergent Culture in Multiplayer Games and Virtual Worlds* (Boston, MA: MIT Press, 2009), and Geoff King and Tanya Krzywinska, *Tomb Raiders and Space Invaders: Videogames, Forms and Contexts* (London: I.B. Taurus), 2006.

31. Industry Facts, Entertainment Software Association, 2014.

32. Ibid.

33. Shaker Milli A, "Rape Is Hilarious, Part 53 in an Ongoing Series," shakesville.com, posted August 12, 2010. Retrieved March 4, 2014.

34. Daniel Kaszor, "Download Code: Penny Arcade Needs to Fix Its Krahulik Problem," financialpost.com, posted June 21, 2013. Retrieved March 10, 2014.

CONCLUSION: PASSING THE TEST

In a 1985 installment of *Dykes to Watch Out For*, a comic strip about the day-to-day lives of lesbians in and around pop culture, Alison Bechdel playfully and insightfully drew up a set of rules that could be applied to works of fiction, particularly movies, so that gender bias could be easily identified. The rules are: 1) it has to have at least two women characters, 2) they have to talk to each other, and 3) their conversation must be about something other than a man. These rules have officially been adopted by film critics, audiences and scholars as the Bechdel Test, and have been applied to a wide range of films, including by a large group of feminist film scholars. Arguably, the real utility of the Bechdel Test is its ability to not simply identify the quantity of females on screen, but the quality of those representations and the relative depth of those characterizations. Since its widespread adoption, the test has been adjusted for depth (that there must be at least 60 seconds of conversation between women, for instance[1]), for race (it has to have two POC [people of color] in it, that talk to each other, about something other than a white person[2]) and applied to other media, including TV and videogames.[3] There is also bechdeltest.com, a wiki-database that has tested over 4,000 films with the added requirement that women who appear in the films must be named characters. But, is there a Bechdel Test for men? To my knowledge, there are only a few half-assed attempts by men out there, trying to be cute or clever, with no acknowledgment of the political purpose of the original Bechdel Test, as in the blog, *Reverse Bechdel Test*: "1) Is there more than one man in the movie, 2) Do they talk to each other, 3) Do they talk about something other than a woman?"[4] And so it is my purpose here to propose a meaningful Bechdel Test for representations of men in the media, men within the margins, by using our knowledge of the other guy and how he has articulated himself throughout this book.

In terms of the first rule, the work of clinical and developmental psychologist James Marcia is both informative and revealing. In, "Ego-Identity Status: Relationship to Change in Self-Esteem, General Maladjustment and Authoritarianism," Marcia distinguishes four distinct Identity Statuses: Foreclosure, Identity Diffusion, Moratorium, and Identity Achievement, usually experienced during adolescence, but often negotiated for the remainder of one's lifespan.[5] In Foreclosure, the person makes identity commitments that are based on external models, without questioning their validity or applicability for their self. Arguably, this is the stuff of traditional male development, where the sons follow in their fathers' footsteps, holding them up as a template for their own identities. However, even if the foreclosure is based on a relatively positive male model, Marcia finds that those stuck in foreclosure have not experienced positive development, as this must always include one's own choices and agency, as well external examples. Marcia also finds that adolescents can also form an identity that is directly in *opposition* to the parent, what he calls "negative identity."[6] Diffusion finds the person making no commitments, their identity diffused and unstructured, which often leads to Identity Moratorium, or an anxious state of searching, for substitutes and other external alternatives. Finally, once the person has undergone a crisis involving a working through or rejection of the above stages, or some shift in personality identification, they reach Achievement, where they make commitments and decisions regarding their idealized, or at least agreed upon, identity. Thus the first rule of the Bechdel Test for Men is that *the work* (film, program, game, etc.) *must have at least one positive male role*, quite possibly an other guy who, even if he is in the process of solidifying his identity status, is open to acknowledging the process itself. While I realize that in many different cultures, a positive male role can mean many different things, he must at least possess a strong empathic sense, engage with others ethically, and actively pursue equality amongst the sexes, genders, races and ages. Throughout this book, we've encountered many different kinds of men, and many different kinds of other guy that seem stuck in the Diffusion or Moratorium stage. Michael Kimmel certainly seems to be describing this male 'kidulthood' in *Guyland*, and Patricia Cohen documents the ubiquity of these stages (in so many terms) in her historical account of the rise of our contemporary conceptions of middle age, in her book *In Our Prime: The Invention of Middle Age*.[7] However, what is important, if not obvious, to note about the other guy is that his synaesthetic masculinity is partially formed from media objects that might often fail the Bechdel Test, but that if he is actively questioning his responses to those films, programs, games, etc., and desires to engage with them (and others in the real) in a meaningful manner, he must question his previous identity commitments. This can be achieved through active and engaged communication that concedes power and recognizes the importance of many voices.

For the second rule, I would like to revisit a theory that I have traced out in the introduction to this book, particularly Mikhail Bakhtin's structural schematic for the human psyche, and its extension, the notion of the dialogical self. In his analysis of the work of Dostoyevsky, Bakhtin finds that there is no single author of Dostoyevsky's novels. Instead, each character inhabits a separate location and commands a singular voice.[8] This is akin to polyphonic music, or a balanced culinary dish, where all of the voices or flavors speak together, substantiating each other while retaining individual qualities. Often referred to as polyvocality, this notion lies at the bedrock of a great deal of postmodern criticism and theory of language, literature, music, art, and culture, as well as larger political and ideological concerns of the functions of representation, identity and community in a globalized world. Substantiated by this theorized polyvocality of communication, the dialogical self is then a psychological figuration where the self comes into being and sustains that beingness through the imagining of other's voices in concert with one's own, as a means of navigating the oppositions between interiority and exteriority. In terms of the other guy, the dialogic self is a naturally useful metaphoric identity schema for his synaesthetic masculinity, as it must constantly incorporate other voices, albeit many of these voices stem from the media (as well as those that surround him in the real). This leads me to the second rule of the Bechdel Test for Men, *that he communicates, without resorting to violence.* As a figurative opposite of empathy, violence is too often the end result of male frustration, acts of domination, fear in the face of waning influence and entitlement, and the inability to account for difference as a progressive and liberating force. Communicating without resorting to violence also means, for the other guy in particular, an eminently achievable strategy for living, one that considers himself as integral to the continuance and support of a polyvocal culture.

The third rule of the Bechdel Test for Men is derived from Eric Anderson's book, *Inclusive Masculinity*, a work based on sociological studies performed in the U.K. and U.S. on the changing attitudes of university men, as well as Anderson's personal observations, performances and teaching. He finds that great shifts in attitude have grown out of the changing cultural landscape, citing "the growing percentage of people who engage in pre-marital intercourse, the social and legal permission for divorce…(and) a lessening of the traditional double standard for heterosexual intercourse."[9] He also cites "the markedly expanded social and political landscape for gays and lesbians" as central to the rise of "inclusive masculinity," a masculinity that shares a great deal with the other guy in its synaesthetic melding of external forces and sources toward the performance of gender, one based on empathy and fluidity.[10] Anderson also finds that the Internet and digital culture serve as key factors in a 21st-century sexual revolution, partially because of the increased visibility of gay and lesbian sexual/social practices, as well as the circulation of LGBTT cultural tropes, that circulate through networks and on our screens. For Anderson, this transferal is part of a series of larger cultural shifts, from exclusivity to inclusivity. At the heart of our current shift is "homohysteria," or straight men's fear of being homosexualized. With the use of this term, Anderson is presumably playing on the problematic baggage attached to the word 'hysteria,' as he identifies his work and position as "social-feminist."[11] In describing "homohysteria," Anderson identifies three key variables:

1. mass awareness that homosexuality exists as a static sexual orientation;
2. a cultural zeitgeist of disapproval of homosexuality, and the femininity that is associated with it; and,
3. the need for men to publicly align their social identities with heterosexuality in order to avoid homosexual suspicion.[12]

These three factors connect cultural homophobic anxiety with individual punitive and policing procedures of others' (and one's own) masculinities. In this sense, Anderson's assertion shares territory with David Savran's brilliant conception, masculine self-reflexive sado-masochism, or the trials that straight men put themselves through in order to purge themselves, and their bodies, of the homoerotic (while also surreptitiously enjoying the pain and gain). From the corporeal penetrative excesses of macho action movies, to the erotics of shared woundedness at the hands of the encroaching minority and feminine masses, the self-reflexive sado-masochist male subject is dying to prove himself, so to speak. For Savran, and perhaps for Anderson as well, straight men are also in the closet, albeit one constructed with lots of hidden panels that lead to other straight men's closets, so that they can rehearse their frenzied mimetic, monolithic and hegemonic performance of masculine straightness while others watch (and so that they may act as voyeurs as well). Here is where the third rule tumesces. Anderson's inclusive masculinity serves as a positive and purposeful account of the changing nature of the other guy, and straight masculinity in general. Certainly, this theory is substantiated by the past decade's metastatic growth of regressive and paranoid masculinities in the U.S.; men who push legislation through state governments requiring the use of vaginal wands as a prerequisite to have an abortion, the flurry of stand-your-ground laws, or the fragmented battle over the rights of gays and lesbians to marry. Progress in social justice often results in a furious backlash, and so Anderson's inclusive masculinity is certainly a good omen, a marker of change, a theory/concept/subjectivity that signifies that progress has been made. The poisonous lie of the current culture wars—that an actual conflict exists between the real, God-blessed Americans in the middle of the country, and the godless heathens on the coasts, points to the merits of exclusivity for some, that the conflict itself will serve as a kind of trickle-down socio-cultural policy. But, it also points to the inclusivity of a mindset that permeates all places and all bodies, a bottom-up model of gender and sexual equality. And so the last rule of the Bechdel Test for Men is: *in a way that promotes gender and sexual parity*. The three rules, taken together, are:

1. It must have at least one positive male role
2. That communicates without ever resorting to violence
3. In a way that promotes gender and sexual parity.

Like the original Bechdel Test, they are neutered if they are applied and then catalogued, and then not used as guides for the *production* of media as a response to public desires and demands. This is, of course, an economic question. Yet, it has been documented by the wonk-analysis website *Five Thirty Eight* that the 1,615 films that passed the Bechdel Test produced in the U.S. from 1990 to 2013 (despite having substantially lower budgets than the median) had a better return on investment than films that failed to include women in a consequential manner. In short, "films containing meaningful interactions between women do better at the box office than movies that don't."[13] Now, if Hollywood can just follow this analysis, as well as hire more women to *make* films…

I am deeply hopeful that the reader understands that I do not equate the other guy's relatively minor marginalization with the deep and problematic oppression of women, minorities, gays, lesbians or any other members of the communities that are forced to the margins. However, I remain optimistic about the other guy's role in conversations and theories of masculinity, visual culture, progressive politics and political change. While I have argued that synaesthetic masculinity is useful as a working model, it is in itself in a type of Identity Moratorium, a mode of searching and anxiety, a self-reflexive palimpsest of inherited masculine excesses. Collective and radical movements as diverse as fifth-wave feminism (as opposed to 'post-feminism'), the Occupy Movement, the Arab Spring uprisings and the anti-bullying movement are all efforts at coming to grips with not only the *presence* of subjugation and violence, but additionally with the *traces* and *fissures* of the historical mechanisms of power. What may prove to be most valuable to the other guys out there, as well as to those of us around them, is their ability to synthesize the presences and absences within themselves, skills they've most likely learned as a result of their tenuous existence between the scene and the screen. The dude abides.

Notes

1. "The Oscars and the Bechdel Test," *FeministFrequency.com*, Feb. 15, 2012. Retrieved April 10, 2014.
2. Alaya Dawn, "The Bechdel Test and Race in Popular Fiction," *TheAngryBlackWoman.com*, Sept. 1, 2009. Retrieved April 18, 2014.
3. John Anthony Agnello, "Something Other Than a Man: 15 Games That Pass the Bechdel Test." Gameological. July 2012.
4. "Reverse Bechdel," *ReverseBechdel.blogspot.com*. No author given. No date given. Retrieved April 14, 2014.
5. James E. Marcia, "Ego-Identity Status: Relationship to Change in Self-Esteem, General Maladjustment and Authoritarianism," in *Social Encounters: Contributions to Social Interaction*, Ed. Michael Argyle (Aldine Transaction, 1973), 340–353,
6. Marcia, 353.
7. Patricia Cohen, *In Our Prime: The Invention of Middle Age*, (New York: Scribner, 2012).
8. Mikhail Bakhtin, *Problems of Dostoevsky's Poetics*, 2nd ed., Trans. R. W. Rotsel, (Ann Arbor, MI: Ardis, 1973).

9. Anderson, Eric. *Inclusive Masculinity: The Changing Nature of Masculinities*. New York: Routledge, 2009, 5.

10. Anderson, 5.

11. Anderson, 14.

12. Anderson, 7–8.

13. Walt Hickey, "The Dollars and Cents Case against Hollywood's Exclusion of Women," *FiveThirtyEight.com*, April 1, 2014. Retrieved April 18, 2014.

GLOSSARY OF TERMS

Brom-com—"Bromantic Comedy"; a subset of a rom-com that features two men's relationship as the central romance, albeit their relationship is platonic; homoerotic undercurrents are often present.

Brony—Originally, a male that is into My Little Pony franchise, but which has morphed into a term that describes any male that is interested in stereotypically female products and pursuits.

Bromance—A seemingly heterosexual relationship between two straight men, often ridiculed by men and women who aren't ready for male emotional openness.

Guy Code—A set of predicate rules and behaviors invented and maintained by straight men as a means of policing their own behavior, as well as a way to distance themselves from women.

Himbo—A male 'bimbo'; a man who is overly obsessed with his appearance and grooming and who is sexually voracious. A potentially misandrous term, but also one that does not acknowledge the sexist nature of the term 'bimbo.'

Kidulthood—A prolonged state of adolescence that can stretch well into one's 30s.

Low-T—A medical problem that men face in their later years, sold by pharmaceutical companies that results in abated sex drive, energy and 'passion for living.'

Man Cave—A refurbished space in a household, often a basement or converted garage, where males gather to drink, eat, play games and socialize away from women. Usually features a bar, beer kegerator, play table, videogame systems and sports memorabilia.

Mancation—A men-only vacation, often to places their partners aren't interested in visiting, such as sports halls of fame, resorts with golf courses, and, of course, Las Vegas.

Macheesemo—A 'cheesy' form of macho, made famous by the male members of the cast of reality-TV show *Jersey Shore*.

Mancom—A relatively new subgenre of sitcom that focuses on the foibles, crises and celebrations of men, about men and for men.

Mandate—A social event enjoyed by men in a bromance, comprised of certain activities (a baseball game or a night out at the bars), but not others (a nice dinner or shopping).

Manscaping—The male act of primping and preening, often associated with the beauty regimens for men introduced on the realty-TV show *Queer Eye for the Straight Guy*.

Mancession—The economic conditions and historical recession of 2008–2012 that put more men out of work than women, and saw more women re-join the workforce as well; see Chapter 1 for details.

Mandom—A Japanese perfume that featured Charles Bronson in their advertisements; like Old Spice, a kind of type of kitschy product that is celebrated ironically by meterosexuals and other guys.

Manfluencer—Men, who, during the Mancession (and beyond) have become the primary purchasers of domestic goods and services (as well as in food preparation and child care), thus their tastes and choices became of interest to marketers and producers.

Manopause—Male menopause, potentially cured by testosterone supplements and other hormone therapies.

Manaissance—The male renaissance. A conflicted term, as a rebirth of men would indicate that they were once more like the other guy, and modern men in general. The term can also refer to a single male, particularly if they are experiencing any type of 'resurgence'—economic, emotional, artistic, etc.

Metrosexual—A contemporary male that revels in fashion, grooming and his appearance, often to the detriment of his other features and skills. Important term in the 2000s, but has fallen into disfavor because of the recession. However, it can be argued that the metrosexual is essentially a European identity, as seen by American men.

Mimbo—Male Instant Messaging boy; a dude who is constantly using his mobile device.

Mumbleguy—A new hipster male, as seen in mumblecore films, often stuck in kidulthood.

No Homo—A phrase a male says to indicate his previous statement was not meant as a 'gay' statement, and that he is straight. Often inadvertently draws attention to the users' homophobia.

Retrosexual—A male who is the opposite of the metrosexual. Often celebrates masculinity of the '50s and '60s, or working class clothing, grooming and attitudes.

Twixter—Someone in their kidulthood, betwixt their teen years and late twenties.

Übersexual—An ideal state of masculinity—the best of the metrosexual, retrosexual and other forms combined. A progressive and a gentleman, educated, tasteful and politically aware, aligned with the feminist project. Can be gay, bisexual, straight or other sexual orientations.

BIBLIOGRAPHY

Adams, Rachel, and David Savran. *The Masculinity Studies Reader*. Malden, MA: Blackwell, 2002.

Agnello, John Anthony. "Something Other Than a Man: 15 Games That Pass the Bechdel Test." Online. *www.Gameological*. July, 2012. Last accessed March 20, 2014.

Alberti, John. "'I Love You, Man': Bromances, the Construction of Masculinity and the Continuing Evolution of the Romantic Comedy." *Quarterly Review of Film and Video* 30 (2013): 159–172.

Aoki, Naomi. "Real Men Exfoliate." Online. *Boston Globe*. April 19, 2005. Last accessed April 2, 2013.

Ashby, Leroy. *With Amusement for All: A History of American Popular Culture Since 1830*. Lexington: The University Press of Kentucky, 2006.

Atkinson, Claire. "He's Tough, He's Soft—He's Complex." Online. *AdAge.com* 75.19 (2004). Last accessed March 17, 2012.

Badinter, Elizabeth. *XY: On Masculine Identity*. New York: Columbia University Press, 1995.

Bakhtin, Mikhail. *Problems of Dostoevsky's Poetics*. 2nd ed. Trans. R. W. Rotsel. Ann Arbor, MI: Ardis, 1973.

Barbieri, Annalisa. "Bags of Masculinity." Online. *New Statesman*.com October 23, 2006. Last accessed June 10, 2011.

Becker, Patricia Vetter. *Shooting from the Hip: Photography, Masculinity, and Postwar America*. Minneapolis: University of Minnesota Press, 2005.

Belk, Russell W., and Janeen Costa. "The Mountain Man Myth: A Contemporary Consuming Fantasy." *Journal of Consumer Research* 25 (1998): 218–240.

Benjamin, Walter. "Unpacking My Library." *Illuminations.* Trans. Harry Zohn. Fontana, London, 1973: 59–68.

———. The Arcades Project. Cambridge, MA: Harvard University Press, 1999.

Berg, Leah R. Vande. "The Sports Hero Meets Mediated Celebrityhood." *MediaSport.* Ed. L.A. Wenner. London: Taylor & Francis, 2002: 134–153.

Berger, John. *The Look of Things.* New York: Penguin, 1972.

Berger, Maurice, Brian Wallis, and Simon Watson, Eds. *Constructing Masculinity.* New York/London: Routledge, 1995.

Best, Amy L. *Fast Cars, Cool Rides: The Accelerating World of Youth and Their Cars.* New York: NYU Press, 2006.

Blazina, Chris. *The Cultural Myth of Masculinity.* Westport: Praeger, 2003.

Bly, Robert. *Iron John: A Book About Men.* Reading, MA: Addison-Wesley, 1990.

Bogost, Ian. *How to Do Things with Videogames (Electronic Mediations).* Minneapolis: University of Minnesota Press, 2011.

———. *Unit Operations,* Cambridge, MA: MIT Press, 2008.

Boon, Kevin Alexander. "Men and Nostalgia for Violence: Culture and Culpability in Chuck Palahniuk's *Fight Club.*" *Journal of Men's Studies* 11.3 (2003): 267–276.

———. "Heroes, Metanarratives, and the Paradox of Masculinity in Contemporary Western Culture." *Journal of Men's Studies* 13.3 (2005): 301–312.

Bordieu, Pierre. *The Bachelors' Ball.* Oxford: Polity Press, 2008.

Bordo, Susan. *The Male Body: A New Look at Men in Public and Private.* New York: Farrar, Straus and Giroux, 1999.

Boyer, G. Bruce. *Rebel Style: Cinematic Heroes of the 1950s.* New York: Assouline, 2006.

Braudy, Leo. *From Chivalry to Terrorism: War and the Changing Nature of Masculinity.* New York: Knopf, 2003.

Breu, Christopher. *Hard-Boiled Masculinities.* Minneapolis: University of Minnesota Press, 2005.

Bribiescas, Richard G. *Men: Evolutionary and Life History.* Cambridge, MA: Harvard University Press, 2006.

Brod, Harry, Ed. *The Making of Masculinities: The New Men's Studies.* Boston: Unwin Hyman, 1990.

Brooks, David. "The Return of the Pig." Online. *TheAtlanticMonthly.com.* April 2003. Last accessed August 3, 2012.

Brown, Ian, Ed. *What I Meant to Say: The Private Lives of Men.* Toronto: Thomas Allen, 2005.

Brown, Patricia Leigh. "The Return of Manly Men." Online. *New York Times,* October 28, 2001. Last accessed July 12, 2013.

Brunsdon, Charlotte. "What Is the 'Television' of Television Studies?" in *Television: The Critical View.* 7th ed. Oxford: Oxford University Press, 2006. 609–610.

Bruzzi, Stella. *Bringing Up Daddy: Fatherhood and Masculinity in Post-War Hollywood.* London: British Film Institute Publishing, 2005.

———. *Men's Cinema: Masculinity and Mise en Scène in Hollywood.* Edinburgh: Edinburgh University Press, 2013.

Buck-Morse, Susan, *The Dialectics of Seeing*. Cambridge, MA: MIT Press, 1991.

Burrill, Derek A. *Die Tryin': Videogames, Masculinity, Culture*. New York: Peter Lang, 2008.

Butler, Judith. *Undoing Gender*. London: Routledge, 2004.

——. *Bodies that Matter: On the Discursive Limits of 'sex.'* New York: Psychology Press, 1993.

——. *Gender Trouble: Feminism and the Subversion of Identity*. New York: Routledge, 1990.

Campbell, Colin. *The Romantic Ethic and the Spirit of Modern Consumerism*. Oxford: Basil Blackwell, 1987.

Chaker, Anne Marie. "Groceries Become a Guy Thing, 'As Men Shop More, Packaging Aims to Win Them Over; 'Inner Abs' Appeal." Online. *WallStreetJournal.com*. Oct. 16, 2013. Last accessed Oct. 20, 2013.

Chakraborty, Barmini. "Market for Men's Skin Care Grows." Online. *Wall Street Journal*. April 20, 2005. Last accessed June 6, 2012.

Chen, Mark G. "Communication, Coordination and Camaraderie in World of Warcraft." *Games and Culture* 4.1 (2009): 47–73.

Chudacoff, Howard P. *Children at Play: An American History*. New York: NYU Press, 2007.

Clum, John M. *"He's All Man": Learning Masculinity, Gayness, and Love from American Movies*. New York: Palgrave, 2002.

Coad, David. *The Metrosexual: Gender, Sexuality, and Sport*. Albany: SUNY Press, 2008.

Cohan, Steven. *Masked: Masculinity and the Movies in the Fifties*. Bloomington: Indiana University Press, 1997.

——, and Ina Rae Hark. *Screening the Male: Exploring Masculinities in Hollywood Cinema*. London: Routledge, 1993.

Cohen, Patrica. *In Our Prime: The Invention of Middle Age*. New York: Scribner, 2012.

Cohen, Robert. *Amateur Barbarians*. New York: Scribner, 2009.

Collier, *Masculinities, Crime, and Criminology: Men, Heterosexuality and the Criminal(ised) Other*. London: Sage, 1998.

Colomina, Beatriz, Annmarie Brennan, and Jeannie Kim, Eds., *Cold War Hothouses: Inventing Postwar Culture from Cockpit to Playboy*. Princeton, NJ: Princeton Architectural Press, 2004.

Connell, Robert. *Gender and Power*. Stanford CA: Stanford University Press, 1987.

——. "Studying Men and Masculinity." *Resources for Feminist Research* Fall/Winter (2001) 43–47.

——. "Masculinities, Change, and Conflict in Global Society: Thinking about the Future of Men's Studies." *Journal of Men's Studies* 11.3 (2003): 249–266.

——, and James W. Messerschmidt, "Masculine Hegemony: Rethinking the Concept," *Gender and Society*. 19.6 (2005): 829–859.

——. *Masculinities*. Second Edition. Berkeley: University of California Press, 2005.

Corbett, Ken. *Boyhoods: Rethinking Masculinities*. New Haven CT: Yale University Press, 2009.

Corrigan, Timothy, Patricia White and Meta Mazaj, Eds. *Critical Visions in Film Theory*. Boston: Bedford/St. Martins, 2011.

Cowell, Maria. "How 'Two and a Half Men' Star Became a 'Paid Hypocrite.'" Online. *Christianity Today*. Nov. 27, 2012. Last accessed January 29, 2013.

Craig, S. *Men, Masculinity, and the Media*. London: Sage, 1992.

Crewe, Ben. *Representing Men: Cultural Production and Producers in the Men's Magazine Market.* Oxford: Berg, 2003.

Cross, Gary. *The Cute and the Cool: Wondrous Innocence and Modern American Children's Culture.* New York: Oxford University Press, 2004.

———. *Men to Boys: The Making of Modern Immaturity.* New York: Columbia University Press, 2008.

Csikszentmihalyi Mihaly, and Eugene Rochberg-Halton. *The Meaning of Things: Domestic Symbols of the Self.* Cambridge: Cambridge University Press, 1981.

Cuordileone, K.A. *Manhood and American Political Culture in the Cold War.* New York/London: Routledge, 2005.

D'Acci, Julie. "Women Characters and 'Real World' Femininity." *Television, the Critical View.* Ed. Horace Newcomb. Oxford: Oxford University Press, 2000: 100–143.

Dawn, Alaya. "The Bechdel Test and Race in Popular Fiction." Online. *TheAngryBlackWoman.com.* Sept. 1, 2009. Last accessed April 18, 2014.

Deveau, Scott. "Lad Mags Last Stand." Online. *National Post.* February 24, 2007. Last accessed July 6, 2012.

Dotson, Edisol Wayne. *Behold the Man: The Hype and Selling of Male Beauty in Media and Culture.* New York: Harrington Park Press, 1999.

Douglas, Edward. "John Hamburg Says I Love You, Man." Online. *Comingsoon.net.* March 12, 2009. Last accessed May 2, 2013.

Duncan, Margaret Carlisle, and Michael A. Messner. "The Media Image of Sport and Gender." *MediaSport.* Ed. by Lawrence A. Wenner. New York/London: Routledge, 2000.

Ebenkamp, Becky. "The Uber-Measure of Man," "Out of the Box," Online. *Brandweek* 46.38 (2005). Last accessed March 25, 2012.

Ellis, John. *Visible Fictions.* London: Routledge, 1982.

Faludi, Susan. *Stiffed: The Betrayal of the American Man.* New York: William Morrow and Company, 1999.

Fausto-Sterling, Anna. "How to Build a Man." *Men's Lives,* 4th ed. Michael S. Kimmel and Michael A. Messner, Eds. Needham Heights, MA: Allyn & Bacon, 1998. 385–389.

Feasey, Rebecca. *Masculinity and Popular Television.* Edinburgh: Edinburgh University Press, 1998.

Fink, Thomas. *The Man's Book.* London: Wiedenfeld & Nicolson, 2006.

Flocker, Michael. *The Metrosexual Guide to Style: A Handbook for the Modern Man.* U.S.A.: De Capo Press, 2003.

Flusser, Alan. *Dressing the Man: Mastering the Art of Permanent Fashion.* New York: Harper Collins, 2002.

Freedlander, David. "The War on Men Author Suzanne Venker, 'I'm Misunderstood!'" Online. *TheDailyBeast.com.* Nov. 27, 2013. Last accessed January 5, 2014.

Fresh Air. Hosted by Terry Gross. "Samberg, Taccone and Schaffer: Three's Not a Lonely Island." Online. *NPR.com.* June 18, 2013. Last accessed Nov. 26, 2013.

Fuchs, Cynthia J. "The Buddy Politic." *Screening the Male: Exploring Masculinities in Hollywood Cinema.* Ed. by Steven Cohan and Ina Rae Hark. New York/London: Routledge, 1996.

Gallagher, Mark. *Action Figures: Men, Action Films, and Contemporary Adventure Narratives.* London/New York: Palgrave Macmillan, 2006.

Garcia, Guy. *The Decline of Men*. New York: Harper Perennial, 2008.

Gardaphe, Fred L. *From Wiseguys to Wise Men*. New York/London: Routledge, 2006.

Gates, Phillipa. *Detecting Men: Masculinity and the Hollywood Detective Film*. Albany: State University of New York Press, 2006.

——. *Hobbies: Leisure and the Culture of Work in America*. New York: Columbia University Press, 1999.

"Gender Equality Universally Embraced, But Inequalities Acknowledged." No author given. Online. *pewresearch.org* July 1, 2010. Retrieved March 8, 2014.

Gibson, James William. *Warrior Dreams: Paramilitary Culture in Post-Vietnam American*. New York: Hill and Wang, 1994.

Gilbert, James. *Men in the Middle: Searching for Masculinity in the 1950s*. Chicago: University of Chicago Press, 2005.

Godeau, Abigail Solomon. *Male Trouble*. London: Thames and Hudson, 1999.

Goldberg, Jonathan. "Recalling Totalities: The Mirrored Stages of Arnold Schwarzenegger." *The Cyborg Handbook*. Ed Chris H. Gray. New York: Routledge, 1995. 233–254.

Goldstein, Richard. "Neo-Macho Man: Pop Culture and Post-9/11 Politics." Online. *TheNation.com* (276) (11) (2003). Last accessed July 7, 2013.

Goodman, Tim. "*Man Up!*: TV Review." Online. *HollywoodReporter.com*. Oct. 11, 2011. Last accessed June 8, 2013.

Grant, Keith Barry. *Shadows of Doubt: Negotiations of Masculinity in American Genre Films*. Detroit: Wayne State University Press, 2011.

Grice, Samantha. "Boys Will Be Boys." Online. *TheNationalPost.com*. April 10, 2004. Last accessed Nov. 15, 2012.

Grose, Jessica. "Omega Males and the Women Who Hate Them." Online. *Slate.com*. March 18, 2010. Last accessed Feb. 4, 2014.

Halberstam, David. *The Fifties*. New York: Villard Books, 1993.

Hickey, Walt. "The Dollars and Cents Case against Hollywood's Exclusion of Women," *FiveThirtyEight.com*, April 1, 2014. Retrieved April 18, 2014.

Hine, Thomas. *The Rise and Fall of the American Teenager*. New York: Perennial, 2000.

——. *I Want That! How We All Became Shoppers*. New York: HarperCollins, 2002.

Hollander, Anne. *Sex and Suits: The Evolution of Modern Dress*. New York: Random House, 1994.

Holquist, Michael, Ed. *The Dialogic Imagination: Four Essays by Mikhail Bakhtin*. Trans. Caryl Emerson and Michael Holquist. Austin: University of Texas Press, 1982.

Holt, Douglas B., and Craig J. Thompson. "Man-of-Action heroes: The Pursuit of Heroic Masculinity in Everyday Consumption" *Journal of Consumer Research* 31 (2004): 425–440.

Howard, Hilary. "For Men: Rub in, Say 'Ahh,'" Online. *TheNewYorkTimes.com* November 19, 2009. Last accessed August 8, 2012.

Hunter, Latham. "The Celluloid Cubicle: Regressive Constructions of Masculinity in 1990s Office Movies," *Journal of American Culture* 26.1 (2003): 71–86.

Hyman, Peter. *The Reluctant Metrosexual: Dispatches From an Almost Hip Life*. New York: Villard, 2004.

"Industry Facts." No author given. Online. *ESRB.com* 2014. Last accessed Feb. 5, 2014.

Interview with Judd Apatow. No author given. Online. *Rolling Stone* 1192, Sept. 26, 2013. Last accessed Sept. 30, 2013.

Jang, C-Y. "Managing Fairness: Reward Distribution in a Self-organized Online Game Player Community." Ed. D. Schuler. *Proceedings of OCSC 2007: Online Communities and Social Computing*. Berlin: Springer-Verlag, 2007.

Jansz, Jeroen. "The Emotional Appeal of Violent Video Games for Adolescent Males," *Communication Theory* 15.3 (2005):219–241.

Jarvis, Christina S. *The Male Body at War: American Masculinity during World War II*. Dekalb: Northern Illinois University Press, 2004.

Jeffords, Susan. *Hard Bodies; Hollywood Masculinity in the Reagan Era*. New Brunswick, NJ: Rutgers University Press, 1993.

Jenkins, Henry, Tara MchPherson and Jane Shattuc, Eds. *Hop on Pop: The Politics and Pleasures of Popular Culture*. Durham and London: Duke University Press, 2002.

Kasson, John F. *Houdini, Tarzan and the Perfect Man: The White Male Body and the Challenge of Modernity in America*. New York: Hill and Wang, 2001.

Kaszor, Daniel. "Download Code: Penny Arcade Needs to Fix Its Krahulik Problem." Online. *financialpost.com* June 21, 2013. Last accessed March 10, 2014.

Kaufman, Michael. "The Construction of Masculinity and the Triad of Men's Violence." *Men's Lives*, 4th edition. Eds. Michael S. Kimmel and Michael A. Messner. Boston: Allyn and Bacon, 1998.

Keen, Sam. *Fire in the Belly: On Being a Man*. New York: Bantam, 1991.

Kiley, Dan. *The Peter Pan Syndrome: Men Who Have Never Grown Up*. New York: Dodd, Mead & Co., 1983.

Kimmel, Michael. *Manhood in America: A Cultural History*. New York: The Free Press, 1996.

——. *The History of Men: Essays on the History of American and British Masculinities*. Albany: State University of New York Press, 2005.

——. *Guyland: The Perilous World Where Boys Become Men*. New York: HarperCollins, 2008.

——. "The Mythical 'War on Men.'" Online. *CNN.com* November 29, 2012. Last accessed March 2, 2014.

King, Geoff, and Tanya Krzywinska. *Tomb Raiders and Space Invaders: Videogames, Forms and Contexts*. London: I.B. Taurus, 2006.

Kusz, Kyle. *Revolt of the White Athlete*. New York: Peter Lang, 2007.

La Cecia, Franco. "Rough Manners: How Men Are Made" *Material Man: Masculinity, Sexuality, Style*. Ed. Giannino Malossi. New York: Abrams, 2000.

Le Breton, David. "Athletic Ordeals: Extreme Sports, Heroism and Virility." *Material Man: Masculinity, Sexuality, Style*. Ed. Giannino Malossi. New York: Abrams, 2000.

LeDuff, Charlie. *US Guys: The True and Twisted Mind of the American Man*. New York: Penguin, 2006.

Lehman, Peter. *Masculinity: Bodies, Movies, Culture*. New York: Routledge, 2001.

——. *Running Scared: Masculinity and the Representation of the Male Body*. Philadelphia, PA: Temple University Press, 1993.

Leland, John. *Hip: The History*. New York: HarperCollins, 2004.

Lhamon, Jr., W.T. *Deliberate Speed: The Origins of a Cultural Style in the American 1950s.* Washington, DC: The Smithsonian Institution Press, 1990.

Lim, Daniel. "A Generation Finds Its Mumble." Online. *NewYorkTimes.com* Aug. 19, 2007.

Lindsay, Greg. "Man vs. Man," Online. *Advertising Age* 76.24 (2005). Last accessed June 13, 2012.

Lombardi, Anna. "Sex Objects." *Material Man: Masculinity, Sexuality, Style.* Ed. Giannino Malossi. New York: Abrams, 2000: 94–100.

Lopez, Mark Hugo, and Ana Gonzalez-Barrera, Women's College Enrollment Gains Leave Men Behind." Online. *pewresearch.org* March 6, 2014. Retrieved April 2, 2014.

Lowry, Toby. "Review: *Man Up!*" Online. *Variety.com* Oct. 16, 2011. Last accessed June 10, 2013.

Luciano, Lynne. *Looking Good: Male Body Image in Modern America.* New York: Hill and Wang, 2001.

Lutz, Tom. *Doing Nothing: A History of Loafers, Loungers, Slackers, and Bums in America.* New York: FSG, 2006.

MacDonald, Jake. *With the Boys: Field Notes on Being a Guy.* Vancouver, BC: Greystone/Douglas & McIntyre, 2005.

Macinnis, Craig. "Macho, Macho Chef: I Want to Be a Macho Chef." Online. *TheTorontoStar.com* August 20, 2006. Last accessed June 28, 2012.

Mackinnon, Kenneth. *Representing Men: Maleness and Masculinity in the Media,* London: Arnold, 2003.

Malin, Brenton, J. *American Masculinity under Clinton: Popular Media and the Nineties' "Crisis of Masculinity."* New York: Peter Lang, 2005.

Malossi, Giannino, Ed. *Material Man: Masculinity, Sexuality, Style.* New York: Abrams, 2000.

Marcia, James E. "Ego-Identity Status: Relationship to Change in Self-Esteem, General Maladjustment and Authoritarianism." *Social Encounters: Contributions to Social Interaction.* Ed. Michael Argyle. Aldine Transaction, 1973: 340–353.

Marwick, Arthur. *The Sixties.* New York: Oxford University Press, 1998.

McCracken, Grant. *Culture and Consumption: New Approaches to the Symbolic Character of Consumer Goods and Activities.* Bloomington: Indiana University Press, 1990.

McDonald, Tamar Jeffers. "Homme-Com: Engendering Change in Contemporary Romantic Comedies." *Falling in Love Again: Romantic Comedy in Contemporary Cinema.* Eds. Stacey Abbott and Deborah Jermyn. London: I.B. Taurus & Co, 2009: 148–159.

Messner, Michael, and Jeffrey Montez de Oca. "The Male Consumer as Loser: Beer and Liquor Ads in Mega Sports Media Events," *Signs* 30.3 (2005): 1880–1909.

"'Mission Accomplished' Whodunit." Online. *CBSNews.com* October 29, 2003. Last accessed November 22, 2012.

"Mission Not Accomplished." Online. *Time.com* June 10, 2003. Last accessed November 21, 2012.

Modleski, Tania. *Feminism without Women: Culture and Criticism in a "Post-feminist" Age.* New York: Routledge, 1991.

Money, John. *Gay, Straight, and In-Between: The Sexology of Erotic Orientation.* New York: Oxford University Press, 1988.

Morin, Rich. "The Disappearing Male Worker." Online. *pewresearch.org* Sept. 3, 2013. Last accessed Feb. 11, 2014.

Morrison, Gary, and Caryl Emmerson. *Mikhail Bakhtin: Creation of a Prosaics.* Stanford, CA: Stanford University Press, 1990.

Moss, Mark. *The Media and Modes of Masculinity.* Lexington, MD: Langham Books, 2011.

Mosse, George L. *The Image of Man: The Creation of Modern Masculinity.* New York: Oxford University Press, 1996.

Nathanson, Paul and Katherine K. Young. *Spreading Misandry: The Teaching of Contempt for Men in Popular Culture.* Montreal & Kingston: McGill-Queen's University Press, 2001/2006.

Neale, Steve. "Prologue: Masculinity as Spectacle." *Screening the Male.* Eds. Steve Cohan and Ina Rae Park. New York: Routledge, 1993. 9–22.

Newell, Walter R. *The Code of Man.* New York: HarperCollins, 2003.

Newkirk, Thomas. *Misreading Masculinity: Boys, Literacy, and Popular Culture.* Portsmouth, NH: Heinemann, 2002.

NPR.com. "The Lonely Island: The Hottest Thing in Fake Hip-Hop." No author given. May 6, 2011. Last accessed Nov. 21, 2013.

Nystrom, Derek. *Hard Hats, Rednecks, and Macho Men: Class in 1970s American Cinema.* Oxford: Oxford University Press, 2009.

TheOnion.com. "Area Man Unsure if He's Male-Bonding or Being Bullied." No author given. Sept. 19, 2013.

"The Oscars and the Bechdel Test." No author given. Online. *FeministFrequency.com* Feb. 15, 2012. Retrieved April 10, 2014.

Osgerby, Bill. *Playboys in Paradise: Masculinity, Youth and Leisure-style in Modern America.* Oxford: Berg, 2001.

Owram, Doug. *Born at the Right Time: A History of the Baby Boom Generation.* Toronto: University of Toronto Press, 1996.

Patten, Eileen, and Kim Parker. "A Gender Reversal on Career Aspirations." Online. *pewresearch.org* April 19, 2012. Last accessed March 7, 2014.

Pearce, C. *Communities at Play: Emergent Culture in Multiplayer Games and Virtual Worlds.* Boston, MA: MIT Press, 2009.

Peterson, Alex. Interview with the Duplass Brothers. Online. *Tiny Mix Tapes.com* July 2012. Last accessed January 16, 2013.

Pope, Harrison G., Katherine A. Phillips, and Roberto Olivardia. *The Adonis Complex: The Secret Crisis of Male Body Obsession.* New York: The Free Press, 2000.

Raphael, Ray. *The Men from the Boys: Rites of Passage in Male America.* Lincoln: University of Nebraska Press, 1988.

"Reverse Bechdel." *ReverseBechdel.blogspot.com.* No author given. No date given. Retrieved April 14, 2014.

Robinson, Sally. *Marked Men: White Masculinity in Crisis.* New York: Columbia University Press, 2000.

———. "Men's Liberation, Men's Wounds: Emotion, Sexuality, and the Reconstruction of Masculinity in the 1970s." *Boys Don't Cry? Rethinking Narratives of Masculinity and*

Emotion in the U.S. Ed. Milette Shamir and Jennifer Travis. New York: Columbia University Press, 2002. 205–229.

Rogin, Michael. *Ronald Reagan, The Movie: And Other Episodes in Political Demonology.* Berkeley: University of California Press, 1987.

Sabo, Don, and S.C. Jansen. "Prometheus Unbound: Constructions of Masculinity in the Sports Media." *MediaSport.* Ed. Lawrence W. Wenner. London/New York: Routledge, 2000. 202–217.

Salam, Reihan. "Masturbation and Solitude: The Adam Sandler Production That Will Save Mankind." Online. *Slate.com* May 19, 2006. Last accessed Dec. 12, 2012.

Salzman, Marian, Ira Matathia and Ann O'Reilly. *The Future of Men.* New York: Palgrave/MacMillan, 2006.

Sanders, Joel, Ed. *Stud: Architectures of Masculinity.* New York: Princeton Architectural Press, 1996.

San Filippo, Maria. Online. *Cineaction.ca* 85, 2011. Last retrieved August 16, 2013.

Savran, David. *Taking It Like A Man.* Princeton, NJ: Princeton University Press, 1998.

Schor, Juliet B. *Born to Buy: The Commercialized Child and the New Consumer Culture.* New York: Scribner, 2004.

Shaker, Milli A. "Rape Is Hilarious, Part 53 in an Ongoing Series." Online. *shakesville.com* August 12, 2010. Retrieved March 4, 2014.

Silverman, Kaja. *Male Subjectivity at the Margins.* London: Routledge, 1992.

Sloan, Bob, and Steven Guarnaccia. *A Stiff Drink and a Close Shave: The Lost Arts of Manliness.* San Francisco: Chronicle Books, 1995.

Smith, Russell. *Men's Style: The Thinking Man's Guide to Dress.* Toronto: McClelland & Stewart, 2005.

Spiegel, Lynn. "The Front Row Is Reserved for Scotch Drinkers." *Television, The Critical View.* Ed. Horace Newcomb. Oxford: Oxford University Press, 2000. 451–469.

Stanley, Alessandra. "Men with a Message: Help Wanted." Online. *TheNewYorkTimes.com* Sunday January 3, 2010. Last accessed July 16, 2012.

Ta, Lynn M. "Hurt So Good: *Fight Club*, Masculine Violence, and the Crisis of Capitalism." *Journal of American Culture* 29.3 (2006): 265–277.

Taylor, T.L. *Play between Worlds: Exploring Online Game Culture.* Cambridge, MA: MIT Press, 2006.

Traber, Daniel S. *Whiteness, Otherness, and the Individualism Paradox from Huck to Punk.* New York: Palgrave MacMillan, 2007.

Tragos, Peter. "Monster Masculinity: Honey, I'll Be in the Garage Reasserting My Manhood." *Journal of Popular Culture* 42.3 (2009): 541–553.

Troyer, John, and Chani Marchiselli. "Slack, Slacker, Slackest: Homosocial Bonding Practices in Contemporary Dude Cinema." *Where the Boys Are: Cinemas of Masculinity and Youth.* Ed. Murray Pomerance and Frances Gateward. Detroit: Wayne State University Press, 2005: 264–278.

Twenge, Jean M. *Where Men Hide.* New York: Columbia University Press, 2006.

Venker, Suzanne. "The War on Men." Online. *FoxNews.com* November 26, 2012. Last accessed Jan. 10, 2013.

Warmelink, Harald, and Marko Siitonen. "A Decade of Research into Player Communities in Online Games." *Journal of Gaming and Virtual Worlds* 5:3 (2013): 271–293.

Watts, Steven. *Mr. Playboy: Hugh Hefner and the American Dream.* Hoboken, NJ: John Wiley, 2008.

Whannel, Garry. *Media Sports Stars: Masculinities and Moralities.* London/New York: Routledge, 2002.

Williams, Raymond. *Marxism and Literature.* Oxford: Oxford University Press, 1977.

Woodward, Kath. *Boxing, Masculinity and Identity.* New York: Routledge, 2007.

Žižek, Slavoj. "Will You Laugh for Me, Please." Online. *InTheseTimes.com* July 18, 2003. Last accessed August 29, 2012.

INDEX

T

This is 40 53, 57–62, 65, 69–74
transgender 29, 117, 130
Twitter 4, 38, 94
Two and a Half Men 94, 119

V

Venker, Suzanne 33, 122–125
victimization 13, 17, 31–32, 68, 92
videogames 3, 6–7, 13–15, 19, 34, 57–58,
        86–89, 91, 108, 112, 114, 120,
        131–133, 141
violence 20, 23, 33, 47–48, 90, 114–115,
        132, 135, 143, 145–146
voyeurism 18–21, 79, 130, 145

W

white masculinity 3–5, 7, 12–13, 17, 21,
        23, 25–27, 30–33, 37–39, 41, 49, 53,
        70, 80, 83–87, 94–95, 99–100, 108,
        111–112, 118, 120–124, 128, 135

Will & Grace 82, 101
World of Warcraft 131
world wide web 6–7, 34, 64, 81–82,
        132–135, 145

Y

YouTube 4, 41, 74, 125

Z

Žižek, Slavoj 97–99

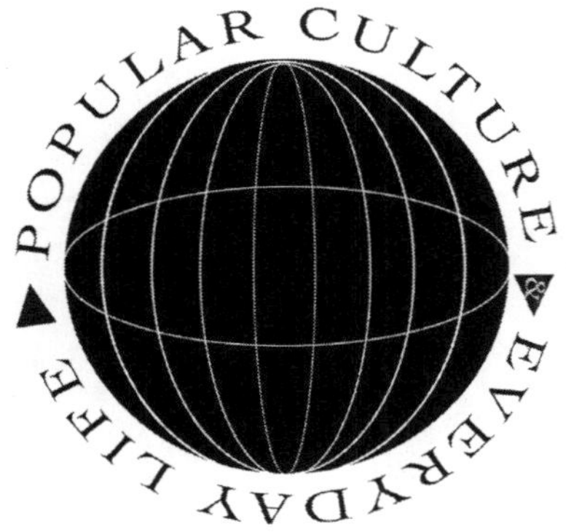

Toby Miller
General Editor

Popular Culture and Everyday Life (PC&EL) is the new space for critical books in cultural studies. The series innovates by stressing multiple theoretical, political, and methodological approaches to commodity culture and lived experience, borrowing from sociological, anthropological, and textual disciplines. Each PC&EL volume develops a critical understanding of a key topic in the area through a combination of a thorough literature review, original research, and a student-reader orientation. The series includes three types of books: single-authored monographs, readers of existing classic essays, and new companion volumes of papers on central topics. Likely fields covered are: fashion; sport; shopping; therapy; religion; food and drink; youth; music; cultural policy; popular literature; performance; education; queer theory; race; gender; class.

For additional information about this series or for the submission of manuscripts, please contact:

Toby Miller
Department of Media & Cultural Studies
Interdisciplinary Studies Building
University of California, Riverside
Riverside, CA 92521

To order other books in this series, please contact our Customer Service Department:

(800) 770-LANG (within the U.S.)
(212) 647-7706 (outside the U.S.)
(212) 647-7707 FAX

Or browse online by series: www.peterlang.com